Governing and managing Church schools

Second edition

Church House Publishing
Church House
Great Smith Street
London SW1P 3NZ

ISBN 0 7151 4992 X

Published 2003 by Church House Publishing

Cover design by Julian Smith and Church House Publishing

Printed in England by
The Cromwell Press Ltd, Trowbridge, Wiltshire

Governing and managing Church schools

Second edition

David W. Lankshear and John R. Hall

CHURCH HOUSE PUBLISHING

Contents

Contents

Contents

List of abbreviations

AMP	Asset Management Plan
ASC	Agreed Syllabus Conference
CEO	Chief Education Officer
CPD	Continuing Professional Development
CRB	Criminal Records Bureau
DBE	Diocesan Board of Education
DDE	Diocesan Director of Education
DfES	Department for Education and Skills
EDP	Education Development Plan
ESP	Education Strategic Plan
GTC	General Teaching Council
ITT	Initial Teacher Training
LEA	Local Education Authority
LMS	Local Management of Schools
NQT	Newly Qualified Teacher
OFSTED	Office for Standards in Education
PSHE	Personal, Social and Health Education
PTA	Parent Teacher Association
RE	Religious Education
SATs	Standard Assessment Tasks
SACRE	Standing Advisory Council for Religious Education
SMSC	Spiritual, Moral, Social and Cultural education
SOC	School Organization Committee
TTA	Teacher Training Agency

Introduction

An important characteristic of Anglicanism is its generous and open commitment to education. Most Anglican parishes offer opportunities for children, young people and adults to learn more about the faith and about themselves. Anglican churches and halls are often used to host educational and cultural activities. Wherever the Anglican Church flourishes, it has created schools and universities or colleges. Usually these initiatives have welcomed pupils and students regardless of their own faith background.

As a reader of this book, you are almost certain to be involved in this Anglican enterprise of education. You may be a governor, a teacher, a member of staff, or a parent at an Anglican school. You may be, or have been, a pupil or student at an Anglican school or college. You may have been to Sunday school, scouts, guides, playgroup or adult education class run in church premises, probably partly funded or subsidized by the church. A great many people in England and Wales have been in contact at some point in their lives with the Anglican Church's educational work. You are probably now making, or planning to make, a significant contribution to this work as a governor or as a teacher in an Anglican school.

This book serves as an introduction to Church schools generally and Church of England and Church in Wales schools in particular. It is designed to help teachers, other staff and governors understand how their work fits into the vision of a Church school as a whole. It cannot be a comprehensive guide. It contains, however, a number of routes into the most comprehensive resource for Church schools that has been produced by the National Society in its 200-year history. The web site to which this book serves as an introduction is available to every Church of

England and Church in Wales school. All the issues in this book are considered in more detail in the Church school management section of the National Society's web site, which can be accessed by using the following address: http://www.churchschools.co.uk. The Church schools management section of the web site is organized so that it is easy to use if you need more information about a topic mentioned in this book. Since the site was launched, it has continued to develop with detailed information on all aspects of the management of Church schools. The book and the web site together are intended to complement and support the help, advice and training available from the diocese.

Every diocese has a diocesan director of education (DDE) with a professional team responsible to the Diocesan Board of Education (DBE) for supporting the work of schools and colleges in the diocese. If you do not know how to contact your diocesan director of education, your school will be able to give you this information or you can contact the National Society.

Before reading the main sections on different aspects of Church schools, it is important to put today's Church schools in their historical context. Many of our schools have their roots in the generosity and foresight of Christians who lived at the end of the eighteenth and the beginning of the nineteenth centuries. At this time there was a great movement to provide formal education for all children in England and Wales, which included initiatives taken by SPCK, the Sunday School Movement, the Welsh Trust, the Gruffydd Jones' Circulating Schools and some enlightened landowners who provided schools for the children of the poor of their parishes. This movement was given focus by two great Church societies: the British and Foreign Schools Society acted on behalf of the Free Churches and the National Society on behalf of the Church of England (which then included Wales). The National Society continues in active support of Christian education throughout England and Wales.

Between 1800 and 1870 most of the schools founded to provide elementary education for the children of the poor were established by the Churches, albeit with some help from government grants to the two Societies and building grants to individual schools. Only after the Education Act 1870 were schools provided by School Boards (from 1902, School Boards were replaced by the new Local Education Authorities). Since 1870 the partnership between Church and State has developed through a series of changes and reforms that reflect the demand for higher standards of educational achievement for all our children.

When the first edition of this book was written the most recent reform was the School Standards and Framework Act 1998, which contained an important reaffirmation of the partnership in education between Church and State.

In November 1998, the work of Church schools was debated at the meeting of the General Synod of the Church of England. Although there were some criticisms of particular events or policies in individual Church schools, no one spoke against the Church's involvement in education or the existence of Church schools within the maintained system. At the end of the debate, the Synod passed the following resolution without a single member voting against it:

That this Synod, believing that Church schools stand at the centre of the Church's mission to the nation:

(a) strongly urge:

(i) Diocesan Synods, in the light of the School Standards and Framework Act, to review the resources available to Diocesan Boards of Education to enable them to be involved in all aspects of statutory education;

(ii) each PCC to discuss how it can serve all schools in the parish;

> (iii) each PCC to commit itself to the greatest possible active support for Church schools in its area;
>
> (iv) each Deanery Synod to consider how it can assist parishes in providing active support for Church schools which serve several parishes within its area;
>
> (b) welcome the opportunities for Church schools to move to the voluntary aided category and encourages dioceses to support governors in so doing, where appropriate; and
>
> (c) invite the Archbishops' Council to review the achievements of Church schools and to make proposals for the future development of Church schools and Church colleges of further and higher education.

In autumn 1999, the Bench of Bishops considered the contribution of Anglican schools to the work of the Church in Wales. They approved the following statement:

> The Bench of Bishops of the Church in Wales:
>
> • Supports the continuing contribution of the Church in Wales to the dual system of education in England and Wales;
>
> • Acknowledges the role of the National Society in enabling this support to be effective;
>
> • Encourages the Church's Provincial and Diocesan Education Officers to develop their work in statutory education in co-operation with the Local Education Authorities and the National Assembly;
>
> • Welcomes the new opportunities presented to the Church in Wales by the School Standards and Framework Act 1998;
>
> • Supports, subject to the decision of the Diocesan Trust, any voluntary controlled school wishing to change its status to that of a voluntary aided school;

- Maintains that Church schools are central to the Church's mission to the nation;

- Invites the whole church community at parochial, deanery, diocesan and provincial level to share in this vision and to promote teaching as a Christian vocation.

These resolutions represented an enthusiastic endorsement and affirmation of the role of Church schools and all who work in them. Following the debate in the General Synod, the Archbishops' Council set up a Review Group, chaired by Lord Dearing and of which Archbishop Rowan Williams was a member, to develop a strategy for the future of Church schools. Their final report, *The Way Ahead: Church of England Schools in the New Millennium*, was published in June 2001.

In the meantime, significant alterations to the funding of capital and maintenance work in voluntary aided schools in England had been negotiated between the Churches and the Government. These changes were enshrined in an Order approved by Parliament in March 2002. In November 2001, the General Synod debated *The Way Ahead* and passed the following resolution adopting the strategies within the report as the Church of England's official policy:

That this Synod ask

- The whole church to build up the relationships described in the report, especially to ensure that Church schools are distinctively Christian institutions, rooted in the life of the parishes whilst being open to the diverse communities they serve;

- The dioceses actively to explore the opportunities for new Church schools, bearing in mind the Church of England's historic mission to serve the whole nation and its special care for areas of social disadvantage and the desirability for such schools to be ecumenically based;

- The whole church at every level to promote the vocation to teach, and in partnership with the Church Colleges of Higher Education to explore ways of supporting the professional and spiritual development of Christian teachers;

- The Archbishops' Council to require each of its boards, councils and committees to discuss the implications of the report for their respective areas of responsibility and to draw up appropriate action plans to implement its recommendations;

- The Archbishops' Council to monitor progress on the implementation of the report's recommendations and to report back to Synod in due course;

And that this monitoring of progress pay particular attention (i) to the enhancement of the distinctively Christian ethos and approach in Church Colleges of Higher Education; and (ii) to the appointment of committed Christian staff in these Colleges where these may be made on the basis of merit for the posts.

In July 2002, Royal Assent was given to the Education Act 2002, which introduced the next round of educational reforms. The first edition of this book was published in January 2000 and has sold out. Since then, there have been a number of legislative changes and developments in Church education policy. Thus, instead of another impression, this is a new edition, which has been extensively rewritten, incorporating significant new material. Education policy and practice change constantly however. This edition has been prepared at the point when many of the regulations that follow the Education Act 2002 have yet to be published. Details of the implications of these regulations for Church schools will be explored on the National Society's web site as soon as possible after the regulations have been published. It seems likely that this edition will need to be replaced in two or three years' time. There is no hope of producing a volume that will stand for all time.

The publication of *The Way Ahead*, the first major Anglican report on schools and colleges for 30 years, is very significant for Church schools and all who work in them. For this reason, every chapter of this book begins with a quotation from the report. Hard copies of the report can be bought from Church House Bookshop and it can be downloaded from www.natsoc.org.uk. An accompanying video, *The Challenge of a Lifetime*, designed to stimulate local discussion of the report, can be borrowed from your diocesan director of education. We hope that this book and the accompanying material will help you to enjoy the work that you do in the Church's schools.

'Church schools', where it is used as a general term in the text, refers to all those schools in the maintained system in England and Wales that have a Church of England/Church in Wales foundation, or where the Anglican Church is a significant partner. This includes many schools in the voluntary and foundation categories. It also includes Academies that are Church of England foundations or that have a relationship with the Church of England, but there are no detailed comments here about such Academies, which are as yet few in number. Many independent schools also have an explicit Anglican foundation or character. They are Church schools and much in this book should be helpful to them but, since the law does not apply to such schools in the same way as to maintained schools, this book does not directly refer to them.

Broadly the book lays out the principles; the web site provides greater detail and the legal references. For example the section on the curriculum contains statements about the different requirements for religious education in different categories of school. If you wish, you can use the web site to check where these requirements are detailed in the law of education. The web site will also alert you to other issues related to religious education, which could affect the situation in a particular school.

Education law changes – between 1986 and 2002 there were 16

Education Acts. The principles on which Anglican schools are organized are more constant. That is why the aim is for the book to deal with these principles and for the web site to deal with the details of the law. Inevitably this book must contain some detail, some of which experience suggests will become obsolete before a new edition. The web site will be regularly updated as far as possible to ensure that it reflects the current state of the law of education.

A word of warning

No publication, however sophisticated, can cover every event and every incident. These materials are not a substitute for seeking advice from your diocesan director of education or the National Society. This book is intended to serve as a general introduction to the governance and management of a Church school.

We publish with the benefit of excellent legal advice, but there will be further changes in education law and there are varying local practices. There may be ideas for improvement that can be incorporated in a third edition. Please help the process of improvement by contacting us.

If you wish to make contact, please write to us at:

The Schools Strategy Team
Board of Education
Church House
Great Smith Street
London, SW1P 3NZ
Telephone: 020 7898 1491
Fax: 020 7898 1520
Email: pat.barton@c-of-e.org.uk

We hope that you find the material useful in your work.

Church House Publishing has published *The Way Ahead*.

For particular information about the quality of education in Church schools you should refer to:

The National Society's Handbook for Inspection under Section 23 (third edition), The National Society/Church House Publishing, 2000

or (for independent schools)

Christian Character, The National Society/Church House Publishing, 2001.

More detail on all the issues raised in the introduction can be found on www.churchschools.co.uk.

The children come first

In offering an invitation to children and young people from all backgrounds to participate in a Christian community, Church schools can provide a real experience of God's love for all humanity. In a Church school, pupils not only learn about religion but they can experience it as a living tradition and an inheritance of faith. Church schools are therefore a unique gift from the Church to an increasingly secular culture. The Archbishop of Canterbury has written:

> Church schools are as concerned as any other school to equip pupils for lives marked by rapid change, global competition and insecurity. But Church schools know in their viscera that this is not just about acquiring skills and good examination results. It is about forming people who have the moral strength and spiritual depth to hold to a course and weather the ups and downs. It is about forming people who know that economic competition is not more important than family life and love of neighbour, and that technical innovation is not more important than reverence for the beauty of creation.

> *The Way Ahead*, paragraph 3.23

A Church school is, or should be, a Christian community, modelled on the archetypal community, God the holy Trinity, bound together by love. Jesus teaches us to love God with all that we have and with all that we are, and to love our neighbour as ourselves. Jesus, the Son of Man, who came not to be served but to serve and to give his life, shows us what that love is like. Those whom God first loves and serves are able to love and serve God and to love and serve their neighbours, with a service that is itself perfect freedom. The starting point is God's mission expressed in Christ. Through its schools, the Church reaches out in the name of God explicitly as part of God's mission to those in need of

God's loving service. So the school is not there primarily to serve the Church or the adults involved with it. What best serves the education of the children and their particular needs drives everything that happens in the school.

Each child is a unique human being made in the image of God. A Church school will be seeking to serve children, because they are unique, made in God's image and loved by him. It longs for the children to grow in the image of God, to be nurtured in the Christian faith and to grow to live the Christian life. But the means of demonstrating God's love for his children is one of service, providing education, not indoctrination or proselytization. And many will be welcome to whom the Christian faith is alien or unknown, children from families that adhere to another faith or that have no particular religious faith. They can be encouraged in their faith or challenged in their lack of faith.

There is nothing inconsistent in a Christian community confident in its own distinctiveness reaching out to include others and learning from others. It was the Samaritan leper, cleansed by the Lord's miracle, who returned to give thanks. 'Were not all ten cleansed?', Jesus asked. And he healed the daughter of the Syro-Phoenician woman at the well. Both of these stood outside the religious community of Jesus and his disciples. But he reached out to them and received from them.

No one is beyond the reach of God's love, although many, sadly, turn away from him. What is true of adults is true of children. Indeed, Jesus teaches us that the kingdom of heaven is for children and those who can become as children. This is not to adopt a starry-eyed view of childhood. Children are not angels.

What adults working in schools must fully understand and witness in their attitudes and behaviour is that, even when children are behaving like little demons, they are still within the scope of God's love and are still of great worth as human beings made in God's image. Christ's command to 'love one another as I have loved you' is a key text for all who work in schools.

Having made some broad statements about the importance and worth of all children we must now turn to some of the detailed aspects of the life of the school as it seeks to serve them.

Spiritual development

Schools have a responsibility for the spiritual development of their pupils and of the community. This is not new. It was enshrined in the Education Act 1944 and restated in 1988. For the last ten years, schools have been inspected on this aspect of the curriculum. This has concentrated minds. More is said elsewhere in the book, but here is a brief Anglican perspective on spiritual development.

The spirit of a person is that person's spark, character, identity. People who are spiritually mature know themselves, what they are capable of, for good and ill, and have confidence in this self-knowledge. Emotions are ascribed to the spirit, so people who are spiritually mature are in touch with their feelings, are able to laugh and cry, to be delighted and moved, to be spontaneous and thoughtful. Balance is a thing of the spirit, so people who are spiritually mature have the measure of things and see them in their proper perspective, know what really matters. Courage is a thing of the spirit, so people who are spiritually mature can handle their fears and act with determination against the odds, can do right when it is easier to do nothing.

People who are spiritually mature, with a deep sense of themselves, know that they are loved by God and so are able to love, know that they are capable of great goodness and prone to great weakness and wilfulness, know how their spirit grows, as they measure themselves against the fullness of the stature of Christ and know how their spirit is refreshed, through their deep encounter with the Spirit of God. People who are spiritually mature, with a deep sense of themselves, are able to reach out to others, to love, to care, to help, to serve, to be faithful, tolerant and patient.

This spiritual maturity develops in people's encounter with God in worship, prayer and stillness, with life, with events, with other people. It develops best as eyes are opened to the height and depth, to the length and breadth of all that is wonderful and amazing in the world. It develops best through experience consciously recollected. It develops best as questions of meaning and purpose are addressed in tranquillity.

The Anglican understanding of spiritual development draws on a rich tradition, from the Bible and from writers on the things of the spirit, throughout Christian history. Part of the work of a Church school is to put pupils in touch with this great inheritance of faith. Just as in intellectual development the school enables pupils to stand on the shoulders of the intellectual giants of the past and does not expect them to start in everything from first principles, so with spiritual development. And the Anglican tradition, drawing on a breadth of insights, Catholic and Reformed, ancient and new, is particularly diverse and rich.

Pupils in a Church school will become gently steeped in the particular part of the Anglican tradition represented by the local parish. But it is proper that they should also be introduced to forms of spirituality outside this experience. These forms may be the expressions of different styles of being Anglican, the practices of different Christian denominations and the practices and beliefs of different faiths. In all this, the approach for spiritual development is one of learning, of being enriched, not one of spiritual tourism or an exercise in human anthropology.

There is a caveat. It is not appropriate to expect pupils to take a full part in activities that are contrary to the beliefs in which they are being raised or to which they hold. They can learn about how other people express their spirituality. They may discuss why this is important to those people. No attempt should be made to force them fully to participate. The issue here is not the legal rights of parents to withdraw their children from RE and school worship, but the respect that the school should be showing for the integrity of members of the school community. It is particularly important that Anglican schools demonstrate sensitivity in this area with pupils whose families are members of other faiths.

Spiritual development is not always smooth. It may entail suffering. It must certainly take account of suffering. Schools need to provide a safe and secure place in which children can work through issues that are distressing or worrying them. This implies that schools are not places in which emotions are suppressed but rather places in which they are acknowledged and given expression. A school where children and adults can laugh and cry together is providing an important emotional support and equipping children to grow into mature adults who are comfortable with their own emotions and sensitive to those of other people. The spiritual development of the whole community, including parents, teachers and other staff, even the governors and those who visit the school, is a proper aim for a Church school.

Moral development

Church schools are often reputed to have good discipline. Another way of looking at it is that Church schools set high store by the moral development of the pupils and of the whole school community. They have a good understanding of the ground and source of moral development in the Christian understanding of God and of humanity.

The word discipline has come to have several meanings in common usage. Anyone becoming involved in a school will need to reflect on what it means in the context of a school. It is sometimes used instead of classroom control. We hear people talk about teachers having good discipline, meaning that they are able to exercise good control in the classroom. Again the word is used to describe the standards of behaviour demonstrated by the pupils: 'The school is well disciplined.'

It is really a misnomer to refer to a school discipline policy. Any policy that focuses only on discipline will fail. An effective policy must include not only a clear understanding of what will happen when things go wrong but also a clear statement of how the school will react when things go well.

The policy must relate to the school ethos statement and, therefore, in Anglican schools it will reflect Christian principles. Within the policy will be a clear statement of how the school will provide an experience of forgiveness and reconciliation when things have gone wrong. This may not be easy to sustain for those children who find conforming to the rules of the school difficult.

All the adults involved with the school must understand the school's policy and apply it as consistently as possible. Teachers will be in the lead on this, but everyone who has contact with the pupils will have a contribution to make. This must include the meal supervisors and other support staff, who are in regular contact with the pupils. The opportunities to provide them with training about their role in the policy and their work with the pupils may be limited, but it is vital that they are taken if there is to be consistency of practice throughout the day.

Another area in which it is hard to establish consistency is the reward system. Too often praise and encouragement come to those who achieve in absolute terms in classroom work, sport or music. Somewhere there must opportunities for pupils who do their best to be rewarded, not because they are top but because they have surpassed their previous best achievement. A challenge to many schools may be, 'How do we encourage and reward our well-behaved triers?' Amongst the strategies for achieving this are personal records of achievement or learning profiles, which seek to identify the whole range of a child's interests, abilities and achievements as well as what they find difficult or challenging.

Many schools have found it helpful to agree certain basic statements about the standards of behaviour expected in the school, together with sanctions that will be applied if these standards are not met. These statements are then well publicized around the school in the expectation that this will promote consistency of behaviour and response. In most schools where this has been tried, it has been found to be helpful. It works well for most pupils, most of the time. Within any school community there are occasions when a pupil arrives at school in a very disturbed state or becomes very disturbed by what he or she experiences in school. For these children conforming to the basic rules becomes impossible. In such cases action needs to be taken swiftly to resolve the situation. A disturbed child needs to be taken out of the class setting and given help and support to enable him or her to return in a better frame of mind. Action like this does not condone bad behaviour, it seeks to prevent it. Swift preventative action also prevents other pupils from perceiving any unfairness in the application of the general rules.

By the time pupils leave school they should have developed into adults who are self-disciplined and who understand and accept that there have to be constraints on behaviour in a civilized society. The school's discipline policy should have this as one of its goals. Governors should be able to identify how that goal will be achieved. One of the elements of such a policy will be giving pupils responsibility, in a safe environment, where failure is not a total disaster but an experience from which to learn. It will be clear that what has been said in this paragraph also relates to the citizenship agenda. As schools introduce citizenship into the curriculum it will become increasingly important that the experience of being part of a school community supports and develops what is being learned in the taught curriculum about being a responsible and participative citizen of a local community.

There are some specific elements within a discipline policy that need to be addressed in more detail.

1. Exclusions: The law allows for pupils to be excluded from school in extreme cases. There is concern that some schools are using this sanction more than is absolutely necessary. Exclusion, where it is used, should be a response either to an extreme incident of unacceptable behaviour or to a long-term catalogue of incidents where all other attempts to bring the behaviour to an end have failed. Sometimes, in the way some schools have used this sanction, exclusion seems to be used as a response to bad behaviour that could have been foreseen or prevented. Periodically, schools should review their policy and practice in the use of exclusion in order to ensure that it is being used appropriately.

2. Corporal punishment: This is against the law and should not feature in any discipline policy.

3. Detention: Pupils may be kept back after school as a punishment but only after the parents have been given notice that the pupil will be late home. Inevitably this means that any detention can only take place some time after the incident that has led to this form of punishment.

4. Home–school agreements are a standard requirement for all schools. They have two specific contributions to make to a discipline policy: they make the basis of the policy open to all parents at the time at which the pupil enters the school; and they provide a basis for the development of individual agreements if the pupil's behaviour within school is being discussed with the parents. This second purpose has a particular importance when a pupil is either in difficulties or has been excluded for a short period and is now being prepared for re-entry into school.

5. Bullying is a particularly difficult problem to handle success-fully. It involves at least four groups of people: the bully, the victim, the bystander and the adults within the community. A discipline policy will contain provisions for dealing with all forms of bullying from physical assault to name-calling and social exclusion. It will address how perpetrators are dealt with, victims supported and bystanders encouraged to be more active in the creation of good relationships between everyone in the community. The policy might have a useful side effect. Some adults lacking good classroom control have been known to resort to bullying pupils. A good anti-bullying policy should prevent this unacceptable adult behaviour.

6. Racism is a particularly unpleasant form of bullying. Every Church school should have a policy that actively addresses racism. This must include presenting positive images of our multicultural and multi-ethnic society, as well as details of the way in which racist incidents will be handled.

Attendance

Every child should attend school on every day that the school is open unless they are too ill to do so or there is urgent need for them to be elsewhere. If a child is not at school a parent should provide an explanation for the child's absence. In these days, when there is great concern for the safety of children, it is helpful if such an explanation is given to the school either before the absence, in the case of such things as hospital appointments, or at the beginning of the absence, if a child is ill. If parents establish a pattern of informing the school before or at the start of an absence, then the school is in a good position to identify incidents of truancy and also those rare incidents that give rise to concern about the child's safety.

There are several possible causes of truancy and schools will need to be prepared to take action to deal with these causes where truancy is an issue. This will need the adults involved to work together in the interests of the child concerned. It is the parents' responsibility to ensure that their children attend school. Action taken to stop individual cases of truancy will, therefore, almost always need to involve the parents. One or more of the following factors may cause truancy:

- problems at school with teachers or other adults;
- problems at school with pupils;
- problems at home;
- peer pressure;
- attraction of activities outside school.

If the school is to take positive action to reduce truancy, it will need to be able to identify the causes of each individual's truancy and deal with them as far as lies within the power of the staff. In extreme cases a child may need to change school or have a special regime of support to enable him or her to make a return to full participation in school. The longer truancy is allowed to run on undetected or unchecked, the more difficult will be the child's return to school.

Truancy, however, is not always about missing whole days or sessions. A subsidiary pattern of truancy occurs in some schools, where pupils miss certain lessons, perhaps taking advantage of split sites or movement between buildings to avoid the most disliked subjects or teachers. Such truancy is best prevented by careful checking of registers at the beginning of lessons to ensure that the whole class is present and by taking action if pupils are not where they are expected to be.

In recent years there has been much pressure on schools to take action to reduce the incidence of truancy and unauthorized absence. There have been well-publicized court actions against some parents who seem unable or unwilling to ensure that their children attend school when they should. Only headteachers can authorize absence. On some occasions they may be approached to authorize absence so that children can take part in family holidays. The provision that permits this type of absence is intended to enable parents who cannot take their annual leave during school holidays to have a holiday with their children. There is anxiety about the potential abuse of this provision. Headteachers should seek to encourage parents to use the school holidays as far as possible, so that absence from school is minimized. This is essential, for while presence at school does not guarantee learning, absence from school certainly reduces it.

There are separate but related issues in some schools over long-term absence during visits to family abroad, in particular in South Asia. A delicate balance needs to be maintained between, on the one hand, the proper wish of many parents with strong family roots and ties in other parts of the world for their children to develop a positive sense of these roots and to get to know members of their wider family in person and, on the other hand, the need for the pupil's education not to suffer through disruption. This balance is not easily achieved but it is the school's duty both to ensure that parents understand the educational loss that will occur through lengthy absence during term time and to work to minimize the actual loss by whatever means.

Intellectual care and safety

Schools should be places where ideas are explored and where individual differences are valued. This implies that pupils must be safe to explore their own ideas. They should be able to do this in an atmosphere which may reject the idea or challenge them to reconsider or explore the consequences of adopting the idea as part of their beliefs, but which never rejects them because

11

of the idea that they are exploring. Two examples will make the point:

1. An eleven-year-old boy was present at an act of worship, which included a presentation based on Genesis 1. At lunchtime he was heard to say to his teacher, 'You don't believe all this rubbish about God making the world in seven days, do you?' Some of his friends displayed shock at this expression of heresy in a Church school. The teacher accepted the comment and required the boy to take his expressed opinion seriously by responding with, 'What do you think?' There followed a lively discussion with the group, which explored some of the possible interpretations of the story.

2. A thirteen-year-old, in the course of a class discussion, made an overt but possibly unintentionally racist statement. The teacher in response made it clear that there were people in the class who would be offended by the remark and asked the pupil to explain why they would be offended. Having been given the opportunity to think through the issue, the pupil was then asked to rephrase the statement in a way that was not racist. Care was then taken to ensure that the other pupils in the group accepted the rephrasing. The idea was rejected; the pupil was not. If the pupil persisted in making racist statements then that would be dealt with within the context of the school's policy for dealing with racist behaviour. The principle here is that pupils should be given the chance to withdraw from unthinking offensive statements or ideas.

Another aspect of intellectual safety relates to peer pressure or bullying focusing on a pupil's ability or lack of it. This is most often stereotyped as the mockery of those who fail to learn as quickly as their peers or fail to acquire a sporting skill as easily. This is only one manifestation of this form of peer persecution. It can also manifest itself in the mockery of those who learn easily or who show real interest or enthusiasm for the material being learned. Being mocked for what you can do is as difficult to deal with as being mocked for what you cannot. Schools need to guard against either of these developments by setting an atmosphere in which everyone is valued and in which pupils undertake such a range of different activities that everyone experiences success and failure and learns to come to terms appropriately with both.

Some educational needs and disabilities

Pupils may have Special Educational Needs as a result of a variety of factors. A Church school will have a particular concern to ensure that special needs, which are part of the child's uniqueness as a human being, meet with a suitable response.

Too often, adults automatically use a deficit model when they consider pupils with special needs. In order to guard against such thinking, the first group of special needs that will be considered will be those resulting from particular abilities.

There will be some pupils in every school who have a particular academic, artistic, musical or sporting ability. How are such pupils challenged to achieve the most of which they are capable? While developing their talents, how can a school ensure that they receive a rounded education?

There will be some pupils in every school who make normal or perhaps very good progress in most areas of school life, but find a particular concept or skill difficult to grasp and master. How does the school ensure that such pupils are helped and encouraged with the challenging aspects of their work? A moment's reflection will reveal that almost every pupil will come into this group from time to time.

There will be a few pupils in every school whose special needs are long term, some of them permanent. There are well-established procedures for identifying these needs and developing a strategy for meeting them within the context of the school. For those whose needs are greatest this will include developing a formal statement. Every school must have a teacher who is Special Educational Needs coordinator and a governor who takes particular responsibility for this area on behalf of the governing body. For some of the pupils within the formal Special Educational Needs procedure, there are issues that are confidential. Governors not involved in Special Educational Needs work must accept that it may not be possible to share all the information about some pupils' needs.

In all schools there will be a need to ensure that buildings are adapted wherever possible to improve the access for pupils or adults whose mobility is reduced. It is important that governors support such projects in order to ensure that they meet their responsibilities for both the children and adults associated with the school. A failure to do so could put the governing body in breach of the duties imposed by the Disability Discrimination Act on all those responsible for buildings to which the public has access.

In all schools there will be a need to provide special equipment or special training for staff in order to ensure that the education of pupils is facilitated. In some cases finance or other resources will come from the LEA, Social Services or the Health Authority. Sometimes the school will meet these needs from its own budget.

Despite the widely accepted policy of greater inclusion in mainstream education, for some pupils there is still a need for special education in units designed for their particularly severe needs. Many of these are based within mainstream schools and thus facilitate integration. A few of these units, probably for those pupils whose needs are so great that only such schools have the resources to provide for them, will be separate from mainstream schools.

There is one exercise that can help governors and managers review their approach to the full range of Special Educational Needs in their school. For each subject area or main activity within the school ask three questions:

1. In this area of the school's life, how would pupils demonstrate that they had special abilities and how would we meet such pupils' needs?

2. In this area of the school's life, what short-term difficulties might pupils encounter, and what action would be taken to help them?

3. In this area of the school's life, what specific long-term learning difficulties might pupils demonstrate, and how would we help and sustain them through such problems?

Try this exercise for mathematics, music and religious education first. What does it tell you about your school?

Physical care and safety

The school will have a number of measures in place designed to ensure that the school is a safe place for children. Every adult who has substantial, unsupervised access to the pupils must be prepared to accept that they will be subject to clearance through the Criminal Records Bureau, under arrangements put in place by the LEA or by the Diocesan Board of Education. This is one of the basic precautions created to ensure that no one who has demonstrated that they might be a danger to children has access to them within the school context. Governors should set an example in this by willingly cooperating in obtaining clearance themselves.

Every adult entering the school premises will be asked to comply with the security arrangements that the school has in place. These will probably include signing in and out and wearing an identity badge while on the premises. The school entrance will be clearly signed from every point of access to the school grounds and all visitors will be asked to report to the secretary's office or other reception point before attempting to visit any other part of the school. Schools in areas where there is deemed to be a higher than normal level of risk will also have other measures in place. Detailed advice on these matters is available to governors and school managers from both the DfES (or Welsh Assembly) and the LEA.

Physical safety is not just a matter of protecting pupils from attack by adults. It has many other aspects. The school will seek to ensure that all its activities are conducted in a safe manner, with precautions in place that are appropriate to the activity being undertaken. This includes the basic assumption that there is always an appropriate level of adult supervision. The governing body will have adopted policies, usually on the advice of the LEA, that set appropriate standards in these areas.

A further aspect of physical safety is safety from other pupils. There is much public concern over bullying in schools. The governors will need to be satisfied that policies, which they have approved, are in place and being observed to combat bullying wherever it may arise. No school can ever afford to be complacent in this area. All need active policies that both deal with incidents when they arise and are designed to prevent their occurrence. While most bullying is perceived to be about pupils bullying other pupils, there are other forms of bullying. Perhaps the most obvious, although rare, is bullying of pupils by members of staff. The governing body must act appropriately, under guidance, to deal with all accusations or incidents of this type.

The governing body now has clear responsibilities for the maintenance of the school buildings. These responsibilities extend to the health and safety aspects of the building, both for children and for staff. In most schools there will be members of staff who have specific responsibility for ensuring that that building is maintained as a safe place in which to work. In some smaller schools the responsibility will fall directly on the headteacher. It is important that the responsibilities are clear and that periodically the school is inspected from a health and safety aspect to ensure that it continues to provide a safe environment.

But schools are not just about the prevention of harm. They should be seeking to be positive over such matters and to promote health. The Healthy Schools initiative is a good example of the way in which a number of strands of policy can be brought together into an approach that provides a positive dimension to this work.

School trips and journeys

At various times while they are at school, children should have the opportunity to take part in visits to places of interest as an integral part of the curriculum. They may also be offered the opportunity to participate in recreational activities as part of a school group. Both these types of activity are an important part of a child's overall educational experience. From the school's point of view, they provide a broadening of the curriculum and an opportunity to know and understand the children more deeply as a result of seeing them in a different context. They also make an important contribution to the social education programme in the school.

Every school trip, whether it is a walk to a local shop with the nursery children or a field trip to a distant part of Europe with sixth-formers, needs careful planning and preparation. There must also be good coordination with colleagues so that pupils are not faced with insoluble conflicts of interest or destructive competition between different departments' activities. The purpose, costs and timing of trips will need to be carefully explained to parents so that they are in a position to make an informed judgement about their child's participation. Where a trip is an essential part of the curriculum, schools will need to establish how they are going to meet the costs, what part of these may legitimately be passed on to parents and how children whose parents cannot afford such costs will be enabled to take part. Where the trip is desirable, but not essential, and is therefore happening outside main school time, it will presumably be self-financing.

Governors will need to be satisfied that the school's arrangements for such trips take full account of the governing body's responsibilities for the health and safety of their pupils and staff. They should be satisfied that there are enough staff on the trip and that they are fully qualified and experienced to lead the activities that are to be undertaken. Where there are specialist activities that are being led by staff at the centre where the pupils are staying, the governing body will need to be satisfied that the centre has ensured that these staff have been properly trained to lead such activities with this age group of children.

The variety of children in the care of the school

The second paragraph of this chapter began with a statement about the uniqueness of each child made in the image of God. The school's task is the same as the task of parents and all those who love each child, to help them to grow truly to be themselves and thus to be able to make their own unique contribution to the development of God's creation. This nourishing of each child's individuality is particularly demanding for schools where children come in classes of 30 or more.

However, recent trends in education, which seem at first sight to militate against the development of the individual, could have the paradoxical effect of encouraging it. Each school now knows its targets for SATs and for other public examinations. The government has set its own targets and individualized them for each LEA. The LEA has its own Education Development Plan and has individualized the targets for each school. Targets may seem to trivialize the education of the whole child, but they certainly avoid the risk of undervaluing basic skills such as literacy and numeracy. The aim of ensuring improvement in these areas, so that no one leaves school in the future unable to read and write, must be supported by everyone in Church schools and by the whole teaching profession. Most schools now individualize targets in these areas for each pupil and keep pupil achievements closely monitored in the light of their own targets. For this they must treat each child as an individual.

Some criticisms have been voiced about the return over the past few years to whole-class teaching. Certainly the literacy and numeracy strategies, which have been seen by most teachers as particularly successful, have demanded some whole-class teaching. Many teachers have found that refreshing. It is, however, particularly demanding for teachers to ensure that each child is participating and developing through these strategies to the best possible extent. There is room for a variety of teaching strategies. The current increase in the number of, and development in the skills of, learning support assistants might mean that small group work in future can always be led by an adult and thus retain momentum.

More pressing than the issue of pedagogical styles is the need to maintain breadth in the curriculum and to avoid a reduction to utilitarianism. Education must not be limited to what can be seen to have a useful purpose. The Latin root of the word suggests a meaning for education close to drawing out from each individual what is in them rather than stuffing them full of knowledge. The classroom should remain a place where breadth and individuality flourish.

This section has focused on the classroom but examples could be taken from every aspect of the school day. The school's first duty is to the child – each one individually. Even when the parents and the teachers are discussing the latest fund-raising proposals, the purpose is still to make the school a better place for the children for whom they share a concern and commitment.

Admissions

Every school must have an admissions policy. It comes into effect if the school is oversubscribed, that is, if a year group for which parents seek admission for their child has already the number of pupils set as the admission number for that year, or if the total number of applicants exceeds that number. The admissions policy must be published in the school's prospectus of information for parents. An admissions policy determines which children will enter the school. It also determines which children will not gain a place. It is hard but sometimes necessary for governors to make these decisions.

In voluntary aided and foundation schools the admissions policy is a matter for the governing body; they are the admissions authority for their school. The governing body determines the policy and a committee of governors makes the decisions based upon it. The committee may have the assistance of the headteacher and other members of staff but the policies are theirs and the decisions are theirs. Every year the governing body must consult with the LEA and with the governing bodies of other voluntary aided and foundation schools on their policy. They must take into account the effect of any changes on other local schools. The Government has indicated an intention to require this consultation only in alternate years unless the governing body intends to change its policy.

In voluntary controlled schools the LEA is responsible for

admissions. It is the admissions authority for all voluntary controlled schools and for all community schools. The LEA will
determine the policy and make the decisions. If the LEA wishes
to make changes, however, it must consult the governing body
about the proposals. In some cases, the admissions policy adopted
by the LEA recognizes the importance of denominational elements
in the admissions criteria. *The Way Ahead* recommended that all
LEAs adopt such criteria.

Following the 1998 Act, most LEAs established Admissions Forums.
The Education Act 2002 made them a statutory requirement in
every LEA. Under the Education Act 2002 LEAs were also given
responsibility for the coordination of admissions procedures in
their area. They have to discuss this role within the Admissions
Forum. At the time of writing it is clear that this coordination
of admissions will require changes to schools' admissions procedures. The biggest change will be that the LEA will receive from
every admissions authority their own decisions about the pupils
to whom they are prepared to offer places and the LEA will notify
parents of the decision. The LEA should not be deciding between
alternative offers, thus undermining the power of the admissions
authorities. To avoid this risk, it seems likely that schools will have
to list pupils in order of preference, rather than simply deciding
whether to accept or reject. The intention is to reduce the
confusion for parents; there may be an added burden for some
governing bodies. In response to questions from the Churches,
the Government made it clear, however, that there was no intention to undermine the admissions authority's power to determine
oversubscription criteria. This may all have become clearer before
you read this. Guidance will be available, of course, from the
diocesan director of education.

The starting point for any school's admissions procedure is the
number of places available. Until recently there has been some
confusion about the way in which this can be calculated, because
different parts of the law of education have, for different

purposes, produced varying ways of calculating the overall capacity of the school. The mysteries, obscure to most people, of standard numbers and admissions numbers and 'more open enrolment' (MOE) measures of the school's capacity, are soon to give way to a new and simpler approach to the calculation.

The next series of decisions concerns those whom the school is called to serve. There is helpful guidance in *The Way Ahead*, which is now the policy of the Church of England. Anglican Church schools are to be distinctively Christian, indeed clearly Anglican, and to help them in this they should, as far as possible, have strong Christian leadership and a solid core of staff and pupils for whom the Christian character of the school is personally significant. Church schools should be places of Christian nurture. The report does not identify the size of the 'solid core', which, in some cases, as far as the pupils is concerned, may be quite small. That is acceptable because Anglican Church schools should also be inclusive of the local community, such as it is, and they will reflect the character of the community. Church schools should be places of Christian service. In inner cities and villages, the Church school is likely to be a neighbourhood school, the school to which everyone sends their children. A village school cannot reject all the non-Anglicans in the village and send them to the nearest non-Church school five miles away, whilst admitting Anglicans from a ten-mile radius. That is not the way. In the suburbs, where there is plenty of choice of primary schools or where pupils are anyway having to travel to secondary schools, a governing body may well decide to give first choice to practising Anglicans and then to Free Church Christians and so on. But some places should be available for children from the immediately local community and some for any children of other faiths whose parents seek, as they often do, an education that understands and respects religious faith and commitment. So there is no one-size-fits-all specification. But there is a clear policy: distinctive and inclusive; nurture and service; reaching out in mission.

In January 2002, the Church of England House of Bishops issued an important statement on this subject:

Bishops commit to inclusive Church schools

Church of England schools must be open to the diverse communities they serve, the House of Bishops says in a statement issued today. Their history of service to the nation's children requires Church schools to be inclusive in admissions, the bishops say, committing themselves to 'ensuring that all Church of England schools should seek to offer places to children of other faiths and of no faith in their local community'.

The House of Bishops statement, agreed unanimously, says:

'Through each of its 4,700 schools, the Church of England is strongly committed to serving the whole community from a distinctively Christian standpoint. Church schools must be distinctively Christian institutions rooted in the life of the parishes and open to the diverse communities they serve. Historically, Church of England schools have been a service to the nation's children and this requires them to be inclusive in admissions, as most already are. We are committed to ensuring that all Church of England schools should seek to offer places to children of other faiths and of no faith in their local community.

'It has been suggested that religious schools are divisive, but we note remarks in the Cantle report on *Community Cohesion* that, because of their location, "non-faith schools can have a very narrow range of pupils based around one culture". We welcome the policy that other faith communities should be invited to sponsor schools within the maintained sector and that these too should be inclusive. We support the suggestions for "twinning" between schools.

'Children in Community schools have the right to experience the living faith of the various faith traditions within our society. All schools, whether rooted in a particular faith or not, need to promote the understanding of other faiths and cultures.'

The Education Act 2002 extended the powers of Diocesan Boards of Education to give advice to governing bodies of schools in the diocese. They should be in a position to give advice over admissions policies and governing bodies are required to have regard to the advice they have been given. They have, of course, relevant experience and they will also have an overview of the schools in the diocese and a diocesan policy about the character of those schools. In this often contentious and important area for schools of all kinds – and for the Church as people scrutinize the Churches' work in education – schools are vulnerable to criticism and challenge. Other admissions authorities may object to a school's over-subscription criteria. This will be dealt with by the Secretary of State for Education and Skills, where the challenge concerns the religious criteria. In coming to a decision, the Secretary of State will be bound to ask what advice was received from the diocesan director of education and how the governing body had regard to that advice.

Framing a school's admissions policy is inevitably difficult and complex, demanding a high level of clarity of thought and a real breadth of understanding of how parents (and sometimes their legal advisers) will read it. Here are some general principles.

- A good policy enables parents to see clearly where they stand. Clarity of wording is important.

- A good policy enables the governing body to draw a clear line between those children it will and will not admit.

- Unless the policy makes it clear that some other rule applies, the order in which the categories are listed is the order in which they must be applied.

- The policy should require statements made by parents to be verifiable by external reference.

- Governors need to make their decisions objectively and in accordance with their published criteria. Where the governors have obtained references or used other external data to make their decisions, these may become evidence if parents decide to appeal against the governors' decision.

The review of the policy by the governing body is only the beginning of the process. They must first consult with the DBE and with the LEA and other governing bodies about their proposals (see above). They should also seek the views of parents. Having carried out the consultation and approved the final version of the policy, the governors should then turn to the admissions application form. It should also ensure that the governing body collects from the parents all the information that it will reasonably need in order to apply the admissions criteria. A good test is to go through the criteria asking:

- Where, in the application form, do we find the information that is needed for each criterion?

- If we are going to take up references, where are we given the names and addresses of those who will provide the references? or

- If the parents are being asked to submit a reference with their application, is it clear from whom they should obtain the reference and what information is required?

- Is there space for the parents to give all the information that we need?

- Is the form clear?

In some primary schools, approaches for places are often received on behalf of very young children. Of course, information can only be given on the admissions policy that is being used at the time of the first approach. It should be made clear that this might have changed before the time when the formal application for a place has to be considered. Parents who seek to apply for a place before the admissions policy for the year in question has been adopted should be told that their application is premature and be sent information about the admissions arrangements at the appropriate time.

Timetable for applications

Within the information provided to parents there should be a clear indication of the timetable for the decision-making process. Local admissions authorities working through the Admissions Forum will have agreed this.

In many primary schools the timetable for applications is complicated by a pattern of entry into school that has children in the same year group starting school at different points in the school year. There needs to be a single process for deciding who will be admitted. Therefore, applications from the whole of the year group will be considered together regardless of their actual start date. This should ensure that the criteria are applied fairly to the whole year group. The decisions should usually be taken at least a clear term before the first children are scheduled to start school. This allows half a term for appeals to be resolved and half a term for the induction programme to take place. Since the Education Act 2002, the timetable has become a matter for the locally co-ordinated admissions arrangements.

The detailed decision-making process is undertaken by a small group of governors acting with the authority of the whole governing body. They need all the evidence available to them and they should act carefully to ensure that they consistently apply the governing body's policy. They must not alter that policy during the decision-making process, even if they come to the conclusion that it needs further review. They must not use evidence that they have not been given formally. For example, in a small community it is possible that some members of the panel know some of the families whose applications they are considering. Governors must be careful to avoid being influenced by this personal knowledge.

Appeals

The existence of the appeals system allows the governing body to make unpopular decisions that they know to be necessary. For the appeals system to work properly the governors of the school must also be undertaking their own responsibilities effectively. Having decided to admit those children whom they believe best match their published criteria, governors need to view any appeals as a useful independent check on their work.

The appeals panel is entirely independent of the governing body and of the LEA. The costs involved are part of the usual expenses of running a school and, as such, should be met either through delegated budgets or from funds identified by the LEA for that purpose.

Appeals panels have two distinct issues to consider as they hear an appeal. First:

- Have the governors correctly administered their published policy in this case?

- Have the governors shown that admitting this child would prejudice the provision of efficient education at the school or the efficient use of resources?

If the answer to both these questions is 'yes', the second issue is a matter of balance between the parents' request for their child to be added to the school roll and the governors' explanation of the impact on the school of an additional pupil.

The appeals panel needs to hear all the appeals for places in a particular school before they decide to admit any child on the basis that this admission would, on balance, not have an excessively adverse effect on the use of educational resources in the school. If the panel feels that the school could admit two more pupils without undue problems, they must then decide which two of the pupils whose parents have appealed will receive the places. They can only do this fairly after they have heard all the appeals.

It is worth noting that different rules apply when a child has been refused admission to school on the grounds that such an admission would breach the restriction introduced in 1998 on infant class sizes (broadly, no more than 30 per class). In this situation the appeals panel can only allow the appeal if it is satisfied that the decision to refuse the child a place was not one which a reasonable admission authority would make, or that the child would have been offered a place if the published admission arrangements had been properly implemented.

While the appeals panel is a formal, independent body, its hearings are conducted in such a way as to put parents at their ease.

Admissions to nursery classes that are part of a maintained school – a special case

Everything that has been discussed about admissions so far applies to children entering school at or shortly before statutory school age. If the school has a nursery class, this raises different issues. There may be historic agreements about the admissions to the nursery, entered into at the time that it was agreed that one would be created at the school. These may allocate a certain proportion of places to children nominated by Local Authority Social Services department for example. Within the Local Authority Early Years plan these historic agreements may have been reviewed or superseded. Where there are no special criteria in existence resulting from such constraints, the governing body is free to establish its own. In practice, it is almost impossible to sustain an admissions policy for the nursery that is different from that of the school in general. Parents do not accept statements that attempt to make it clear that a place in the nursery does not guarantee a place in the school. In one respect, however, the law is different. Parents have no right of appeal over the governors' decision not to admit their child to the nursery.

The National Society/Church House Publishing has published:

Spiritual Development in Schools, Brown, Alan and Furlong, Joan, 1996

Feeding Minds and Touching Hearts, Brown, Alan and Seaman, Alison, 2001

Moral Education, Ainsworth, Janina and Brown, Alan, 1995

Respect for All, Griffith, Daphne and Lankshear, David, 1996

which all relate to issues raised in this chapter. There is also relevant material in:

The National Society's Handbook for Inspection under Section 23 (third edition), 2000

and (for independent schools)

Christian Character, 2001.

More detail on all the issues raised in this chapter can be found on www.churchschools.co.uk.

There are no schools without parents

We have also noted that through the children attending its schools, the Church has an opportunity to reach out to parents. The 900,000 children provide access to parents, very many of whom would otherwise have no contact with the Church.

> The diocese of London said in its evidence: 'The Archbishop of York, as Bishop of London, was fond of pointing out that clergy will meet far more family members in a school than they are likely to encounter in Sunday services.'

As of necessity adults will increasingly be engaged in the practice of lifelong learning. If Church schools can become family learning centres in response to this development, so also the opportunity to reach out to parents will be enhanced.

The Way Ahead, paragraph 3.8

If the primary concern of schools is the individual child, then that quickly brings the school into a close relationship with the parents of that child. In this chapter the term 'parents' will be used to cover a wide range of individuals and circumstances. Some children have only one parent living with them. Some will have several adults who care for them and are involved in their nurture and are concerned for their future. The school will see some of these parents regularly, others hardly at all. It is a great mistake to assume that an unseen parent is an uncaring parent.

Parents are the primary educators of children. Schools must work in partnership with parents wherever possible. Good partnerships start with good communication, mutual trust and respect. It is for schools to take the initiatives that create these conditions.

Schools must plan their relations with parents carefully. Teachers and others, particularly office staff, who communicate regularly with parents, all need to understand what type of relationships the school is trying to establish with parents and how they, as professionals, contribute towards them. This chapter will consider a number of points of contact with parents, all of which are significant in the establishment of good relations between the school and the children's parents.

First contact – the school prospectus

For many parents the first formal communication from the school will be the school prospectus. There may have been informal contact with the headteacher or the school secretary in order to obtain it, and those conversations will have begun to set the tone for future relations, but the first formal statements will be in the prospectus. It is not surprising that many schools have put much effort into the production of these prospectuses. Even so, many schools fail to check the legal requirements concerning them. There is a detailed list of the required contents of a school prospectus. Governors need to satisfy themselves that those preparing or reviewing the school prospectus have checked the legal requirements recently and have ensured that they are all met. They can be found on the DfES web site.

At the time of writing, although there are additional requirements for secondary schools, the legal requirements for all schools are as follows:

- the name, address and telephone number of the school;

- the type of school;

- the names of the headteacher and chair of governors;

- information about admissions;

- a statement of the school's ethos and values;

- details of any affiliations with a particular religion or religious denomination, the religious education provided, parents' right to withdraw their child from religious education and collective worship and the alternative provision for those pupils;

- information about the school's policy on providing for pupils with Special Educational Needs;

- pupil absence rates;

- a summary of the national curriculum assessment results in the school and nationally.

The legal requirements are the minimum that the school prospectus should contain. The governing body should also establish what it wishes to see in the prospectus, to help parents to gain an accurate picture of the school. In particular, Church schools will wish to make the links between the school and the Church community clear. Pictures may help to convey a good image; advertising or sponsorship may help pay for the costs of production but the key question must always be 'how does this prospectus help parents to understand the school and what it offers their child?' It may be worthwhile asking someone outside the school community to check a draft of the text for them with this question in mind.

Home–school agreements

Every school must create a home–school agreement. The governing body must consult with parents on the content of the agreement and a copy of it must be provided to every new parent when their child is first offered a place at the school. Where there is a pre-school meeting with parents this may provide a good opportunity to explain the agreement. Schools must ensure that they deliver their side of the agreement. This implies that all members of staff know what is in the agreement and how it affects their approach to their work. Parents cannot be required to sign the agreement as a condition of their child being offered a place at the school, nor can there be any attempt to make its terms binding on them. They can, however, be encouraged to sign the parental declaration. The agreement will lay out the school's expectations of parents and pupils as well as how the school will provide for the child's education in partnership with the parents. This should assist and promote good relations with parents, as it will avoid some of the misunderstandings that lead to breakdowns in relationships.

The basic agreements may also be helpful when situations arise that are creating a cause for concern in the behaviour or attitude of a particular child. Renegotiation of the agreement or a clarification of its principles may form part of the discussion with the child's parents designed to develop a joint strategy between the parents and the school to achieve an improvement in the situation.

Communication

Communication between home and school is often a cause of difficulty and frustration. Many factors are involved. These include:

- the telephone manner of the staff in the school office, including the headteacher;

- the linguistic style used in letters home by individual teachers or by the school clerical staff;

- the differences between the language registers used by teachers and by parents;

- the style of leadership adopted by headteacher, teachers or governors at meetings for parents;

- stress levels;

- the accuracy of what is said at the school gate;

- the extent to which pupils are able to facilitate or hinder communication (e.g. through the 'pupil-post' system);

- the level of confidence with which some parents approach written communications, particularly if English is not their first language;

- parents' previous experience of schools, particularly as a pupil.

Not all of these factors are within the control of the school. Some are unconscious habits that may have to be studiously unlearned.

There are some communications that are so important that they must be sent by post. It is unlikely that any school, for example, would be so unwise or insensitive as to send an exclusion letter home by pupil-post or email. But the Government has been consulting about whether it is appropriate for schools to begin sending 'letters' to parents by email with a view to allowing most communications to be sent by these means. It would only be possible, of course, where parents have volunteered their email address and can reasonably be expected to access their messages on a regular basis. Many schools take pride in having an attractive web site with appropriate links. A Church school site should have links to the parish church and diocesan web sites.

The school staff and governors must take the initiative to ensure that communications are always of the best. It is reasonable to hope that parents will respond to the school's best efforts with understanding and courtesy, but it cannot be guaranteed. This is not an excuse for the school to give up making the effort to communicate well. Governors who are prepared to meet with parents or other members of the community, to explain to them what the school is doing and why, have much to contribute to the school in the development of good communication. Governors who join the parents in pressurizing a school for change may not always be assisting the cause of good communication.

One final thought on communication. Teachers, even head-teachers, do not often have cause to contact the school from outside during working hours. As a result they may be unaware of the impression given to callers over the telephone. The governor who compliments the school secretary, in the hearing of the headteacher, on his or her manner with callers can make a major contribution to the reinforcement of good practice in the school.

Annual report and meeting

The governing body of every school must prepare an annual report for its parents. The annual report must contain all the items required by law. These include details of the action plan following any inspection of the school (under Section 10 or Section 23 of the School Inspection Act 1996) and the latest test or examination results. The report is, however, the governing body's account of their work for the year. This will mean that there are always likely to be items in the report that are not required by law, but which are important to the school.

It is important that the governors are active in the preparation of the report and in its presentation to the parents. This presentation is given at the Annual Parents' Meeting. It is good practice for the chairs of governing body committees to present the section of the report that relates to the work of their committee. This not only makes the presentation more interesting, but also gives parents a feel for how the governors exercise their responsibilities.

Parents must be provided with written notice of the date of the Annual Parents' Meeting. In those cases where it may not be clear how many people should be regarded as a 'parent' of a particular child, the definition provided in section 576 of the Education Act 1996 is used to form the basis of any decision. For voluntary controlled schools, the LEA will make the decision as to whether a person is to be regarded as a parent of a registered pupil. In a voluntary aided or foundation school, the governing body makes the decision. This can be important on those rare occasions when there can be a vote at the annual meeting. In general terms these meetings are an opportunity for governors and staff to involve the parents in the life of the school and to answer any questions that parents may have. The meetings complement, but should not seek to duplicate, the regular meetings between class teachers and parents, when the progress of their child or children can be discussed. The subjects discussed at the annual meeting should be general ones. Discussion of individual teachers should never be allowed. Wherever possible, it should be clear to parents that there will be interesting and important issues to discuss, so that as many parents as possible are encouraged to attend. It should not be assumed that low attendance indicates that everything is well with the school or that high attendance indicates that there is dissatisfaction.

Informal social work

For many headteachers, one aspect of the maintenance of good relations with parents is both demanding of time and professionally challenging. There are many parents who, having confidence in the school, use the headteacher and, sometimes, other members of staff as a source of advice, help and good counsel. This derives from the knowledge that problems within the family setting have potentially a significant impact on the children's ability to profit from their schooling. Within certain limits, therefore, headteachers become involved in the worries and concerns of the family.

The headteacher is not always the focus of the work. In most primary schools the headteacher will be the member of staff most often involved, although other staff may also contribute. In secondary schools the pastoral staff are more likely to be involved. In some schools, the school secretary will fulfil the role for some parents. While acknowledging this, this section will, for brevity, continue to discuss the issues as if it were always the headteacher who undertakes the task.

What are the limits?

Ideally the headteacher should be in a position of a listener who can then point those who need it in the direction of appropriate sources of help. In Church schools this will include the parish priest as well as other professionals.

Ideally the headteacher only becomes involved to the extent that it does not interfere with his or her duty to the children in the school's care.

Ideally the headteacher should not become so personally involved in the issues that it affects his or her personal or home life.

The emphasis on 'ideally' in the statements is intended to acknowledge that the best of intentions do not signify much when a parent arrives at the school at five to nine in the morning in a flood of tears announcing that their partner has left the home taking all the family money but none of the debts. Well-ordered schedules for the day's work are put aside in response to the human need of the moment. At the end of the day the head may be in need of someone with whom to talk through the experience. Good resolutions about not becoming involved will have been discarded.

What can be done?

The school needs to acknowledge that responding to incidents such as the one sketched out in the preceding paragraph are part of the school's task. Some thought can then be given to enabling this aspect of the work to be done as effectively as possible.

- The school should have, readily accessible, the contact names and telephone numbers for the local offices of the various agencies who offer expertise, guidance or support across a wide range of problems.

- Support for the headteacher should be well managed. Where possible, supplies of tea or coffee should be made available. The opportunity to complete the interview with the parent in privacy and without interruption should be facilitated by other members of staff, who can ensure that the telephone is answered quickly and that those wishing to speak to the head-teacher on non-urgent topics are encouraged to find another time for the discussion.

- All members of staff should observe confidentiality on these incidents.

- The headteacher should have someone who can provide a debriefing service if this is needed. There is nothing sophisti-cated in this. What is needed is a good listener, not involved in the school or the immediate community, who is prepared to listen while the headteacher talks through what has happened and how it has been handled.

None of these measures solves the problems, but they may help to keep them in perspective. One final point may also help. If governors and colleagues know that this work is done, they should be able to offer support and appreciation without having to be told any details that would breach the trust that the parents have placed in the school.

Parent Teacher Associations (PTA) or 'Friends of the School'

Every good school will have an organization that brings together parents, teachers and sometimes the supporters of the school from the wider community. The organization may be fairly formally structured or it may operate very informally. What is right for one type of community at one point in time may not be right for the same community ten years later or the next-door community now. From time to time such organizations can become restricted in practice to a small group who, from its own point of view, seems to be doing all the work and, from other people's point of view, seems to operate as a cosy clique. The time is ripe for a change and relaunch.

The prime tasks of such an organization will include:

- support for the school, including but not exclusively fund-raising;

- enhanced communication and partnership between staff, parents and the wider community;

- social and educational activities for parents and families associated with the school.

The PTA may be involved in other tasks, but these seem to be at the heart of such organizations.

Parent Teacher Associations or similar organizations will need to have an established formal structure if they are to raise funds. There are model constitutions available from the National Confederation of Parent Teacher Associations (www.ncpta.org.uk). Whatever structure is adopted, it should make clear:

- how the committee is elected;

- how the committee's membership will be regularly renewed;

- how the purposes of the organization are defined;

- how it will organize its financial affairs;

- how the organization can be wound up;

- how the organization will relate to the governors and, in a Church school, to the parish church.

One of the problems facing anyone trying to write about parents is the plural. Parents, like children, are individuals made in God's image, who are attempting to bring up their children to the best of their ability. In contrast to the school's stance towards pupils, which will be impartial, every parent will be partial for his or her children; that is, they will take their children's part. It is no good expecting parents to be impartial – to understand both sides; they want the best for their children. They expect the school to provide this, particularly if they have chosen the school themselves rather than leave the choice to chance – the school with a vacancy or the nearest to their house.

Teachers and other members of the staff of the school need to build up an atmosphere of trust, collaboration and partnership between themselves and parents. Where this is created there is a reasonable prospect of harmonious working together in the interests of the child, at least some of the time.

Parents are not always correct in their judgements, of course, nor do they always nourish realistic dreams of what their children will achieve in school or in the world beyond. Sometimes schools will need to protect children from the pressures that parents put on them. Occasionally, teachers may need to sustain the child's dream in the face of parental opposition. Rarely, teachers may have to help to protect a child from abuse by parents. Parents are not always right. They do not always know best. Teachers are not always right either. They do not always know best. The same may also be said for governors and for all other human beings. In the main, all of us will try to do our best and sometimes we may even succeed.

The rights and responsibilities of parents

Parents do have rights within education law and it is important that the school honours these. Some of these rights affect the curriculum; others are concerned with their relationship with the school, the teachers and the governors. They can be summarized like this:

Everyone who is a parent, whether the child lives with them or not, has the same right to participate in decisions about a child's education and receive information about the child. However, for day-to-day purposes, the school's main contact is likely to be the parent with whom the child lives on school days.

School and LEA staff must treat all parents equally, unless there is a court order limiting an individual's exercise of parental responsibility. Individuals who have parental responsibility for, or care of, a child have the same rights as natural parents, for example:

- to receive information, e.g. pupil reports or summaries of inspection reports;

- to participate in activities, e.g. vote in elections for parent governors;

- to be asked to give consent, e.g. to the child's taking part in school trips;

- to be informed about meetings involving the child, e.g. a governors' meeting on the child's exclusion.

The welfare of a child will be the paramount consideration for schools. However, where a parent's action or proposed action conflicts with the school's ability to act in the child's best interests, the school staff should try to resolve the problem with that parent but should avoid becoming involved in the conflict.

41

To balance these rights, parents also have responsibilities. The responsibilities include:

- ensuring that their child attends the school regularly and on time;
- collaborating with the school to ensure that their child obeys reasonable school rules and completes tasks set for homework;
- collaborating with the school on measures for the security of all pupils and staff.

The key principle within all these rights and responsibilities is that in any good school there must be a well-developed partnership between the staff of the school and the parents. Without such partnerships very little that is positive can be achieved.

Representation

There are two distinct issues contained in this section. One is how parents can make representations to the school over issues that affect only their children or a small number of others. The second is how parents can make their views known on general issues of school policy and organization.

In the first instance, there needs to be a well-established pattern of meetings with teachers and appropriate levels of school management to ensure that there are good, open relationships and that any issues that arise can be dealt with speedily and effectively. A key point in such a process will be the opportunity that parents have to meet and discuss the issue with the headteacher. Regardless of the size of school and the accessibility of the headteacher, the meeting between parents and the headteacher has formal significance. If the issue cannot be resolved at such a meeting, the options that are open to parents to take the matter further inevitably generate formal action and processes. Parents have the right to take the complaint forward to the governing body if they are not satisfied with the response they have received from the headteacher.

On the more general issues of parents being represented within the formal structures for the governance and management of the school, they are represented on the school governing body through their elected representatives and, in voluntary aided schools on occasions, by those foundation governors who must also be parents. It is important that the school ensures that all parents are kept informed of the names of their representatives so that they can make their views known to them.

Home–school transport

The issues that arise around the journey to and from school are quite complex. They derive from the concern to ensure that all pupils can get to and from school in a safe and appropriate manner. In 1944 certain assumptions were made about the distances that children of different ages could walk safely. These have been clarified by subsequent judgements in the courts. Over the years, public perception of what is appropriate and safe has changed but the legal definitions have not.

For Church schools the issue also involves the extent to which the appropriate school for the child may be a Church school, even when this is not the nearest school.

For Local Education Authorities the issues of cost are important. The provision of coaches and taxis every day to ensure that all pupils arrive at school on time and are delivered safely home at the end of the school day creates a complex administrative task with a significant cost element. This is particularly important for those pupils who have to be transported to special schools or units, where specially adapted vehicles and trained escorts may have to be provided.

Local Education Authorities must provide free transport to school for those pupils under eight who live more than two miles from their school and for those over that age who live more than three miles from their school. Local Education Authorities may choose to provide transport to the nearest Church school, if pupils travel to a school further away than the nearest, where this is beyond the travel limits for children, when the parents adhere to the faith or denomination to which the school is affiliated. Most Local Education Authorities have done this for many years. In setting their admissions policies, the governing body will need to be aware of the Local Education Authority's policy on this issue in order to avoid setting up expectations among parents that will not be met.

Several government initiatives in recent years on the issue of home to school transport have aimed at reducing the traffic congestion caused in many areas by the 'school run' and also the perceived growth of car dependency amongst school children. These initiatives have usually focused on the creation of safer walking and cycling routes to and from school. They are important because the method used to reach school each day will set up habits amongst children that are difficult to break later in life. It is important that young people learn to walk and use bicycles or public transport both for their own health and to reduce pollution and traffic congestion. Many schools have taken useful local initiatives in response to the work that has been done by central and local government.

The National Society/Church House Publishing has published:

Children and Bereavement, Duffy, Wendy, 1995

Children and Divorce, Smith, Roger and Bradford, John, 1997

which are both useful resources for those involved in 'informal social work'.

More details of all the issues raised in this chapter can be found on www.churchschools.co.uk.

Staff: the most important resource in the school

Teachers feel undervalued in our society. The respect that was once theirs is often hard won and too often lacking. Where this is so, it undermines their authority and effectiveness in the classroom and their standing with parents. It bears directly on the willingness of people to enter the profession and on the retention of those already in the profession. **This is an issue for the whole nation. But it is one that can and should be tackled by the Church. Church schools should stand out as places where teachers and other staff are valued and respected. The headteacher should be able to look to the parish church as a source of unfailing support and encouragement.**

The Way Ahead, paragraph 6.5

The staff of a Church school are its most important asset. Next to the pupils they are the most important people in the school. Through them the educational objectives of the school are delivered. They share with the governing body the task of preserving the school's identity as an Anglican school. All teaching and other staff must be aware of their role within the overall policy and ethos of the school. All new staff will require induction into the school traditions. All will require induction, training, support, management, leadership, direction and opportunities for further development. This chapter will consider the principles underlying the employment of support staff, contract staff, teachers and the leadership team within the school. They apply to all categories of Church school.

Employment

Support staff

Within this general category fall all those staff of the school who are not teachers. Some will be employed on an hourly or part-time basis. Some will be full-time employees. Some will need specific qualifications and experience to undertake their responsibilities. Some will simply need a willingness to undertake the task and the personal qualities appropriate to it. Without them the school could not function.

In voluntary aided and foundation schools the governing body is the employer of all the staff within this category except, in some cases, kitchen staff and those employed by contractors. While governors may develop their own policies with regard to their staff, they must work within the framework of employment law. This means, in particular, that they are not able to discriminate on religious grounds on the employment of these members of staff. Staff should know that they must act in accordance with school policies, provided that these policies are not themselves a form of hidden discrimination. All the staff who are employees of the governing body will need a contract of employment that specifically reflects that fact. The National Society produces forms of contract for support staff in voluntary aided and foundation schools. Governors need to be satisfied that those responsible for administering these contracts are completing them in accordance with the guidance provided by the Society. This is also important for part-time staff and those who will only be working during term time.

In voluntary controlled schools the LEA is the employer, but many of the employment functions will be delegated to the school. The governing body must act within the policies laid down by the LEA in the appointment of support staff, and should seek the advice of the appropriate department if they are in doubt. They must not act in ways that exceed their delegated powers under Fair funding. The contract of employment should make clear that in law the employer is the LEA.

Staff employed by others to carry out work in the school on contract

This section deals with the specific issues that arise when the school enters into a contract for services with an 'outside' contractor. The essence of this group of staff, which might include cleaners, kitchen staff and ground maintenance workers, as well as employees of builders, is that they are not employed by the governing body or the LEA. Before any contract is awarded to a contractor it is important that the governing body, the school leadership and the contractors have a clear understanding of how the staff undertaking the work will be expected to conduct themselves. If they are to have unsupervised access to children the contractor must be able to provide evidence that the appropriate Criminal Records Bureau (CRB) checks have been carried out.

Should there be concerns about such staff, either in terms of their performance or their conduct towards pupils or staff, these issues will need to be dealt with in accordance with previously agreed procedures. It is essential that neither school staff nor governors interfere with the established patterns of management. This can lead to confusion and in some cases increased costs. It is important to ensure that employees of contractors engaged in work that can affect the general ethos of the school are appropriately trained to understand their role. Great care needs to be taken in this area in Church schools. The headteacher should be prepared to work with the manager of the contractor's staff to ensure that everyone understands what is required of them. Although the most obvious example of staff in this category are those involved in making, serving or supervising school meals, this group of employees may be engaged on a variety of tasks within the school. The issues are basically the same for all.

Teachers

In voluntary aided and foundation schools the teachers are employees of the governing body. The LEA provides the finance through the delegated budget and, in most schools, may provide payroll services. Since this need no longer be the case, it is no longer, if it ever was, appropriate in voluntary aided schools to refer to the division of responsibilities between the governing body and LEA as that between employer and paymaster. The LEA has an important advisory role, as does the diocesan authority, over matters of employment, but the governing body needs to ensure that it has proper protection in law. As the employer, the governing body must have contracts of employment with teachers in voluntary aided and foundation schools. The National Society produces forms of contract for all teaching staff in voluntary aided and foundation schools. Governors need to be sure that those responsible for administering these contracts, whether the clerk to the governing body, the LEA's personnel service or another provider, are completing them in accordance with the guidance provided by the Society. This guidance can be found either in the series of booklets on staffing issues published by the Society or on the web site. As the employer, the governing body must also have its own policies and procedures for the employment of staff. It is not enough simply to assume that the LEA will have appropriate policies that can be applied. If the governing body has not considered and adopted such policies on the basis that they are suitable to their school, they cannot expect to be fully protected under the law.

The law explicitly gives the governing body of a voluntary aided school the right to choose, in the appointment of teachers, candidates who can demonstrate that they are actively and personally committed to the faith of the school. The governing body needs to have a clear set of policies over how they will use this right in any particular appointment to the school's teaching staff. They should make their intentions clear in both their advertisements and the person specification they send out to interested parties. This right enshrined in section 60 of the School Standards and Framework Act 1998 is not undermined by the Human Rights Act nor is it expected to be by forthcoming anti-discrimination legislation.

In foundation schools the governing body does not have the same power to choose teachers of their own denomination (but see below: reserved teachers).

In voluntary controlled schools the teachers are the employees of the LEA, although many of the functions of employer are delegated to the governing body. In all teacher posts except reserved teachers, the governors must follow the employment policies of the local authority. Only in the specific area of the appointment of reserved teachers may they explore the candidate's suitability to teach religious education in accordance with the teachings of the faith or denomination of the school. Reserved teachers, a special feature of foundation and voluntary controlled schools with a religious character, enable religious education to be taught in accordance with a diocesan rather than an LEA syllabus (see pp. 93–4), where parents so request. The governing body will need to have established a clear under-standing of how a Church school approach to RE is given particular expression in its school at the present, in order to be able to assess the suitability of a candidate for a post that carries the responsibility of a reserved teacher. No more than one fifth of teachers (counted to include the headteacher) at a foundation or voluntary controlled school can be reserved teachers and the headteacher cannot be a reserved teacher.

All schools with a religious character have established an 'ethos statement' (see p. 85). This should form part of the information sent to all candidates for teaching posts. Since they have chosen to teach in a school with a religious character, it is perfectly reasonable to expect them to give active support to the ethos of the school. This applies to all categories of Church school.

Headteachers

The headteacher is the key appointment in any school. All studies of successful schools identify the role played in the school by the headteacher as being critical. The most important contribution that governors can make to their school is to appoint the right headteacher.

In all schools the appointment process for headteachers will be based on the important provisions in education law (section 60 of the School Standards and Framework Act 1998) designed to help governing bodies make the best possible appointment in a Church school. These take account of equal opportunities and human rights legislation and, alongside relevant anti-discrimination legislation, should inform the governing body's equal opportunities policy.

In voluntary aided schools the headteacher is an employee of the governing body. Normally the governors will be looking to appoint a very successful teacher, able to give effective leadership to the school and with a strong commitment to the Anglican Church. Sometimes a candidate who is actively involved in another Christian denomination will be the best candidate, but it is difficult to see how someone without a strong Christian commitment can provide the Christian leadership necessary for the school to be a good Church school.

All candidates for the post of headteacher should be able to demonstrate that they have made a thorough professional preparation for the post. This will include completion of the National Professional Qualification for Headteachers, but on its own this will be sufficient only rarely. Good candidates will have taken advantage of one of the opportunities provided by dioceses, Church Colleges or the National Society to study the specific issues that distinguish Church schools from community schools.

In foundation and voluntary controlled schools the appointment of a headteacher cannot take account of personal religious commitment in the same way. However, the governing body, whether they are the employers (foundation schools) or working under delegation from the LEA (voluntary controlled schools), have the explicit right under section 60 of the School Standards Framework Act 1998 to assure themselves that the headteacher they appoint is fit and able to preserve and develop the religious character of the school. Candidates will give evidence of this both by their professional preparation and by their answers to questions about the professional issues involved in leading an Anglican school. It will be important for governors to distinguish carefully between asking candidates about their personal beliefs and asking them about their professional competence and atti-tudes. It is the latter that should be explored with every candidate. This will include their approach to the headteacher's important role in leading collective worship in an Anglican school and their understanding of the spiritual development of pupils in an Anglican school.

Chaplains/chaplaincy

Some schools have a specifically appointed school chaplain. The employment/appointment arrangements for such posts vary considerably. In some places the appointment is made by the diocese in consultation with the school and may be held by a priest, who divides his or her time with a parochial appointment in the area. In other places the chaplain may be a member of the teaching staff and combining chaplaincy duties with a teaching commitment. In many primary schools the role is undertaken as a voluntary service by the local parish priest or a member of the parish ministerial team. Sometimes the role is undertaken by a group or committee drawn from the staff of the school. Many variations and combinations of these arrangements are possible.

The duties undertaken by the 'chaplain' are almost as varied as the arrangements for employment. They will include a contribution to the organization and leadership of worship and may include a contribution to the pastoral care and spiritual development of pupils and colleagues. As has been implied above, some chaplains may also have a teaching role. Chaplaincy in a Church school is important and how it is given practical expression will be tailored to the needs of the individual school and the resources (human and financial) that are available.

The appointing process for all staff

The governing body's policy for all appointments must ensure that a number of basic steps are taken. These are detailed in the guidance booklets and on the web site. In summary they include:

1. selecting those who will be making the appointment;

2. delegating to those making the appointment the authority to do so;

3. contacting those persons who have a right to attend for the purpose of giving advice (e.g. from the LEA or DBE) and involving them in the planning;

4. drawing up a job description when it is a new appointment, or amending the job description as necessary;

5. drawing up a person specification when it is a new appointment, or amending the person specification as necessary;

6. checking that the application form will elicit the information

needed (if the form is from the LEA, that it is designed for the category of school in question) and does not contravene the governing body's equal opportunities policy;

7. ensuring that the budget can cover the costs of the appointment;

8. establishing a timetable for the appointing process;

9. advertising (internally or externally, in the LEA bulletin and/ or newspapers);

10. arranging for candidates to visit the school and ask questions about the nature of the post;

11. drawing up a short list of those candidates who fulfil all the essential criteria in the person specification and, if appropriate, narrowing down through the use of the desirable criteria;

12. ensuring that the interviewers can be present at the whole of the interviewing and decision-making process.

Each of these steps could be further broken down into sub-steps. Some may appear to be so standard or routine that they are obvious. Each needs to be completed. The National Society can provide examples of incidents where failure to complete each of these individual steps has led to subsequent problems or challenges.

Once all these steps have been completed, the school will be in a position to conduct the part of the selection process in which the most appropriate candidate is finally selected. The interviews should be conducted by members of the governing body or by the head or other members of the school leadership team to whom have been delegated the necessary powers.

During the interview every candidate should be asked the same basic questions, though the use of supplementary questions to draw out a reticent candidate cannot, of course, be subject to the same restriction. The questions should relate to the job description and person specification prepared by the governing body. Governors should ensure that, if they do not possess the specialist knowledge necessary to frame appropriate technical questions and evaluate the answers, they have an adviser or specialist with them to assist with the interview process. This will be particularly important for all headteacher posts and some other senior posts, including heads of subject departments. Time should always be given for the candidates to ask their own questions of the panel and to make sure that the candidate would accept the job if it were offered.

Governors should ensure that notes are kept of each interview – preferably by more than one of the interviewers. Sometimes it is helpful to provide prepared forms for note-taking, which help interviewers to relate what is being said to the requirements of the post.

Formal interviews are not the only nor are they sometimes seen to be the best means of selecting the most suitable candidate. If candidates are to be invited to give a presentation, the available technology will need to be agreed in advance and the time to be allowed for the presentation carefully monitored. The same would be true of an in-tray exercise or a group discussion. It would rarely be possible to ensure that all candidates have an equal opportunity to demonstrate their abilities if they were to be asked to teach a class under observation, nor would it be fair to the pupils, so this method of assessment is discouraged. Care also needs to be taken if there is a desire to seek opinions from potential colleagues; it should be absolutely clear that such opinions cannot be taken formally into account (the colleagues will not have seen anything like the picture the panel has seen) and generally the seeking of such views is discouraged. By the same token, too great a reliance on references is discouraged. They are inevitably partial and should generally not be circulated in advance and should only be used to confirm the panel's judgement once it has come to a view.

When the interviews are complete the interviewers should proceed to evaluate the candidates' suitability and potential. Steps should be taken to ensure that those who are making judgements do so carefully and make full use of the criteria that have been established for the post. It is unfair to all the candidates if any of those making the decisions uses information other than that contained in the application or elicited during the interview. If any of the candidates is known personally to the governors (other than, for example, through being an internal candidate) this knowledge should be declared. Conscious efforts should be made to ensure that such knowledge is not used to influence the decision. There is a special need for care if one or more of the candidates is already working in the school. It is very important that internal candidates are given the same interview experience and are judged on the same criteria as external candidates. This should take account of the particular stress of the interview for all candidates; not all will perform at their best, so it would be unfair to say of a candidate known to the panel, 'I know she can do better than that', when such judgements cannot be made of all candidates.

Someone from the interviewing panel, usually a person with specialist knowledge of the post, should be prepared to offer unsuccessful candidates comments on their performance during the interview. This requires skill and sensitivity. The 'feedback' process is intended to help unsuccessful candidates to learn constructively from the experience. It is usually most helpful once there is some distance between the experience and the feedback, enabling reflection and balance to be restored.

Governors must agree with successful candidates for school leadership the point on the salary scale for remuneration. All those involved in these negotiations on behalf of the governing body should be aware of the school pay policy and the budgetary and personnel implications of any departure from the agreed policy. The clearer that the governors can be on this issue when the post is advertised, the easier are subsequent discussions likely to be. Governors must avoid being trapped into discussing the remuneration package from scratch after the post has been offered and accepted.

Before an announcement can be made, even informally to colleagues, the necessary criminal record checks should have been undertaken and letters exchanged.

Development

It is very unlikely that anyone appointed to a new post has all the skills that will be necessary to undertake their duties effectively in their new setting without some initial support or training. Every new member of staff needs to find his or her way into work in a new setting, within a new policy framework and with new colleagues. For this reason it is important that there is a good programme of induction in place in every school. The need for effective continuing professional development (CPD) for all teachers is increasingly recognized. The General Teaching Council in its first two years laid heavy emphasis on this need of a professional workforce and over the next few years teachers' entitlement to CPD should develop into clear expectations of annual time committed, as in other professional bodies. But the need for appropriate training extends to all school staff and, incidentally, to members of governing bodies.

Induction

The first few days in a new post can be challenging and confusing even for an experienced professional. It is very important that there are good arrangements for the induction of any new employee. This applies whether the employee is the headteacher or the cleaner. The principles are the same. Anyone joining the staff needs to learn about the layout of the buildings, key school policies that will affect them and their work, the overall management structure of the school and how they will personally fit into it. They will need to meet key colleagues. They will need to feel that they are welcomed into the school and that people are committed to supporting them in their work. For many posts it will be appropriate to ask someone to act as a mentor for the first few weeks or months to ensure that the new employee has continuing support and makes the best possible start in the new post. For headteachers a mentor may be a serving headteacher from another similar school (preferably a Church school) within a reasonable distance.

Being a mentor is a major professional responsibility. Good mentoring can help a new employee feel part of the team quickly. It can help them reach an effective level of professional performance as soon as possible. Poor mentoring can lead to disillusionment and alienation. Good mentors are able to provide appropriate levels of support, information and encouragement in equal proportions. They also provide guidance on the way in which the school or the authority is organized and how individuals can extract the best from the institution and work at their best within it. There are no quick guides for mentors on how they are able to achieve this. Essentially they have to develop their role as an interaction with the individual whom they are mentoring.

For teachers in their first year of teaching after qualification (newly qualified teachers or NQTs), special arrangements apply. These are laid out in guidance and now involve the General Teaching Council (GTC), as the body that keeps the register of all teachers. Those responsible for appointing such teachers must be certain that the proper arrangements have been made to ensure that newly qualified teachers make the best possible start in their chosen profession. There is clear guidance available from the GTC about the successful completion of an induction year and the steps to be taken if an NQT is demonstrating inadequate levels of competence for the work. Every effort needs to be made to help NQTs (and qualified teachers for that matter) overcome any areas of incompetence but, ultimately, neither the education of the nation's children nor proper respect for the teaching profession is well served by incompetent teachers.

For teachers who are coming to work in a Church school for the first time it is important that they are helped to understand what this will mean in theory and in practice. A command of the technical details of what makes a Church school different is not necessary for teachers outside the school leadership team but all new members of staff should at least understand the important role of worship in a Church school and how they can and should appropriately bring the Christian faith of the school to life in the classroom. It would be useful if they had undertaken the Church Colleges Certificate in Church School Studies, or its equivalent, as part of their professional preparation for their new post. If they have not done so this could be offered as part of their induction process (see below).

Continuing development and support

Even when the individual has been successfully inducted into a new post, the need for support in it does not end. Staff will need continuing opportunities to develop their skills. This implies that training must be a continuing process throughout a person's service in the school. Involvement in a continuing programme of training is important for the individual's professional development and for the school's continuing improvement. Some of the training may derive from the appraisal process. All will relate to the school's Educational Development Plan (Education Strategic Plan in Wales).

Training is as important for support staff as it is for teachers, so there will be no one in the school whose training needs will be neglected. Governors should be aware of the development in training opportunities open to teachers. The Teacher Training Agency and the National College for School Leadership have developed a range of training appropriate to a series of stages in a teacher's career. These stages include induction, subject leadership, preparation for headship and programmes for newly appointed and experienced headteachers. Teachers preparing for or at these stages in their careers should be encouraged to take part in these schemes. The Church Colleges, working with the National Society, have developed award-bearing courses specifically related to the needs of teachers working in Church schools. These courses can be followed either by attendance at lectures or through distance learning. These colleges have also developed a certificate programme of training for governors. More information on the Church College awards schemes is available from the National Society, from any of the twelve Church of England/ Church in Wales Colleges of Higher Education or from the diocesan director of education.

Support for staff goes beyond the provision of training, however. It includes effective leadership and management, both from the school leadership team and from any other colleagues who have leadership responsibilities. Governors also contribute to the development of the school, by their policies, by the setting of realistic but challenging targets and by their general interest in the school. Governors will need to ensure that they act in concert with the school leadership, so that employees perceive that they are led and managed consistently and fairly.

One aspect of good management is concern for the long-term career development of staff. Promotion, internal or external, will be a key aspect of career development as will training, study and skill development. The governing body has a part to play in these issues, as it will be called upon to set policies and to make decisions that affect the careers of the staff of the school. It is necessary for governors to understand the patterns of career development open to staff in their school. Some career moves need careful preparation; some involve an element of risk taking. It is the task of the school leadership to provide guidance and encouragement to individual employees within the context of the school programme of performance management. Governors need to support this process. Sometimes, particularly in primary schools, the next move in the career and professional development of a teacher will involve a change of school. It is helpful if governors recognize that this is the case and do not seek to discourage teachers from a commitment to their own careers even if this means their school losing an exemplary teacher.

An important aspect of good staff management will be the establishment of an appropriate, fair and affordable pay policy. Governors have limited discretion on the salary and benefits that can be provided for their staff. The policy must stay within the limits set by law and by the LEA Fair funding scheme.

Another aspect of support for staff is the conditions in which they are required to work and the extent to which the school buildings represent a good environment. Governors should do their best to ensure adequate staff facilities. For example:

- Is the staff room large enough to accommodate all the adults who may need to meet for their breaks or for a staff meeting?

- Are the facilities in which the staff work in good condition and well cared for?

- Do those staff who need space to interview people in private have access to appropriate rooms?

- Do those staff who need to store specialist equipment or to change for specialist activities have the facilities they need? Are they adequate for their purpose and well maintained?

Much publicity has been given in recent years to the need for schools to ensure that their security systems are adequate. Staff need to know that they are able to work in an environment where they are as secure as possible from the threat of attack, and that they can summon help quickly should they feel threatened. The measures that the governing body needs to take in any particular school will depend on a careful risk assessment exercise on their school, taking account of advice from the Health and Safety Executive and the Department for Education and Skills. If there is a local school watch scheme governors should consider ensuring that their school is a fully participating member of the scheme.

If people have became more aware of safety issues in schools they must also be aware of concerns over the 'bureaucratic burden' on teachers. Schools must be well administered and, of course, teachers have a part to play in that administration, but it is very important that they are enabled to undertake their main role properly. This means that schools must ensure that they use appropriately skilled staff for the different tasks that must be completed. A school should not be organized in such a way that teachers feel forced to undertake tasks that could be done, perhaps even better done, by other people with different skills. Governors will be aware of this issue when they are making policy decisions about staffing and about the workload that they create for teachers by their own ways of working. As money becomes available it may well be more appropriate for governing bodies to develop a staffing structure with more learning support assistants and other support staff than to seek to increase the number of teachers in the absence of rising school rolls.

Finally in this section there are two issues that will have a particular resonance for Church schools. The first is the area of pastoral care and concern for all members of staff. Sometimes there will be circumstances, perhaps within the personal life of a colleague, when an individual member of staff needs a significant level of support and understanding in order to come through a crisis. Responsible staff will need to act with sensitivity and flexibility in such circumstances. A failure to handle one incident of this nature appropriately will quickly have an impact on a whole range of staff attitudes. 'They wouldn't even let me have time off to go to my mother's funeral', if true, can undermine years of work to generate a family atmosphere within a school.

The second issue is the concern for the spiritual life and development of staff members. Raising this issue should not be taken to imply that schools should be attempting to provide everything that is needed for the spiritual development of the staff. It is, rather, the assumption that Church schools will accept the logic of the argument that suggests that, if the school is committed to the spiritual education and development of its pupils, one of the ways of doing this is to show that the adults in the school take this area of their own life seriously. Governors might ask themselves how their school demonstrates its care for the spiritual life of its staff. What does the school do? What does it facilitate? How is the interest shown?

Appraisal

An important part of any system of staff support is appraisal. Regular meetings to review progress and needs with a senior manager should help staff to maintain a proper view of their performance and value as professionals. This is not just an issue for teaching staff.

There is a national framework for teacher appraisal from which LEAs have developed their own schemes. LEA schemes should include appropriate provision for Church schools. Governors need to be clear about the way in which appraisal operates within their school. They need to be satisfied that all staff have had appropriate training in the appraisal system that is in use in the school. The governing body also needs to ensure that the process is properly supported by an allocation to ensure that any identified training need can be met. This is a key factor in a satisfactory appraisal process. If the result of an appraisal process is the identification of a training need that is not subsequently met, all that has been achieved is to deskill the person being appraised.

The appraisal of headteachers is of particular importance for two reasons. First, it sets the tone and standard for the appraisals of the rest of the staff. Secondly, it is more complex as it will involve external appraisers. In a Church school one of these external appraisers, at least, should have personal experience of work in a Church school. For many members of staff the Church school ethos and their contribution to it will be an important aspect of the appraisal process.

One of the governors, nominated for this purpose by the governing body, will receive reports on the appraisal process from the headteacher. These reports are provided so that the governing body may be assured that the appraisal process is being monitored effectively. It also means that there is a governor who can speak on the issue of staff training and development needs when the governors are discussing the school budget.

Other governors may be asked to provide evidence to the appraiser, when their responsibilities mean that they work closely with the headteacher or other teacher who is being appraised.

The National Society and a number of dioceses have taken steps to ensure that there are publications and training opportunities for teachers and other staff working in Church schools, which can be used as part of a planned follow-up to appraisal.

Performance management

A related but distinct issue is performance management. All Church schools will need to be implementing the formal aspects of performance management. They will be seeking to do this within the overall context of their church foundation and their commitment to providing the best possible education in the name of Christ. Where appraisal is usually understood as a process of review and development for the individual, performance management is focused on a continuing need for the school to enable its employees to work at their best level.

Discipline, grievances and competence

In this short introduction to the many issues that arise in any situation when one of these procedures is likely to be used, the focus will be on general principles. Should any head or chairperson feel that a situation is likely to develop in their school, they should seek the advice of their diocesan director of education immediately, and certainly before any decisions are taken. Too often difficult situations have been made worse by people trying to act without first taking advice.

All staff should have signed a contract that contains a procedure to be used in cases where discipline, grievance or competence issues arise. One of the important aspects of this contract is that it should accurately reflect the employment arrangements in the school. Some of the arrangements for dealing with employment issues will be changing as a result of the Education Act 2002. Details of these changes will be found in the specific guidance on employment issues published by the Society. Those changes will affect the way in which disciplinary decisions are made in the first instance, but the member of staff's right to appeal will not be affected. The appeal will normally be heard by a committee of the governing body. In voluntary aided and foundation schools this is because the governing body is the employer, and in voluntary controlled schools it arises from the arrangements for local management of schools where staffing issues are delegated to the governing body if the school has a delegated budget. In an Anglican school there will be a significant tension for the governors and senior staff of the school in the rare instances when these issues will arise. They will wish to ensure that all staff maintain the highest standards. They will also be concerned that the pastoral needs of all those involved in the situation are responded to appropriately. It is not normally possible for the same person both to be active in the hearings and to provide pastoral care for one of the other parties. Governors will want to be satisfied that arrangements have been put in hand for the pastoral support of all individuals while they deal with those areas of the situation that are their responsibilities as employers. Diocesan directors of education should be asked to provide advice and guidance on all matters to do with these hearings. They can be particularly supportive in assisting the governing body to work through the tensions between the need for formal proceedings and the pastoral care of all the individuals involved in the process.

One of the most difficult problems facing governors in any of these situations is that of being able to demonstrate that they have been fair to all parties. If they have discussed the issues before any hearing they could be perceived as having prejudiced their judgement. It is hard for governors who are concerned for and involved in their school to accept guidance that says, 'The governing body should not discuss this issue at this time, as there could be a formal hearing related to it at some point in the future'. It is, however, essential that they do accept such advice, if it is given.

It is also important that after a hearing those involved in it do not discuss the result or the content with their colleagues on the governing body. There may have to be an appeal and, therefore, a need for governors to be available who have not yet heard the arguments on either side.

Once an issue has been decided by the process, it is essential that all parties stick closely to any agreements that have been made. It is usually helpful for there to be an agreement about what will be said, if anything, to staff, parents, press or the general enquirer. No one in the governing body or the school leadership should deviate from such an agreement. This can be particularly important if there is significant local or press interest in the issue.

Staff absence

Members of staff may be absent from the school for a number of reasons. These will include attendance at meetings and courses as well as absence related to health issues. For the person responsible for ensuring that every class has a teacher, any absence is inconvenient. For teachers asked to cover for absent colleagues, any absence is costly in terms of time that has been committed to other activities. It is very important that absence is monitored and appropriate steps taken to reduce the impact of absence to a minimum.

Five different types of absence related to health issues may be identified. They each call for a different response. All present challenges to the school.

1. *Normal sickness*, that is, short periods of absence resulting from infections, accidents or other cause within the hazards of everyday life. Except during periods of epidemic, schools normally cope with these occurrences, if not with ease, at least with efficiency. One problem faced by many schools is that many staff, knowing the potential disruption caused by any absence, come into work when they should have remained at home. This can delay their return to full fitness.

2. *Repeated absenteeism*, that is, when a member of staff has a series of short periods of absence, beyond that which can be put down to 'normal sickness'. Staff absence needs to be carefully monitored so that absenteeism can be identified and

appropriate action taken. It may be that such absence is a symptom of excess stress or anxiety. Action to reduce the stress being experienced by the member of staff may improve attendance.

3. *Maternity/paternity leave.* There is a legal framework for such leave, and schools must comply with the law suitably and with some flexibility, to meet the particular needs of staff members.

4. *Long-term sickness* resulting from a medical condition which, once diagnosed and treated, should result in a full recovery being made. These issues will arise from time to time in every school. It is clearly helpful to the school if the member of staff can ensure that the school is informed of the likely length of absence that will be needed to complete the recovery. This information will need to be reviewed from time to time.

5. *Chronic illness* resulting from a permanent condition. There are many teachers who work very effectively while suffering from such conditions. Occasionally they may need a short time away from work for treatment or because the condition has temporarily become worse. Some chronic conditions deteriorate over time. In such cases, where it becomes clear that it is no longer possible for them to continue to work, it may be possible for them to retire early on the grounds of ill health. In such circumstances the school will need to act supportively and with great sensitivity.

All of the above comments assume that the absences are brought on by life chances. A tiny minority of teachers have adopted a lifestyle that leads to absences from school. Stereotypically, those who abuse alcohol would probably fall into this category. Head-teachers will need to act positively to ensure that such teachers do not become a burden on the school. Advice on these issues should always be sought before action is taken in individual cases.

Leaving and retirement

Schools are not just responsible for staff while they are employed at the school. They should be concerned and interested in them after they leave. Two examples will serve to illustrate the point.

- 'Do you remember Mrs Smith who used to work here? Well she is a headteacher now!' A teacher with great professional promise begins her career at the school. After a few good years' work within the school she is promoted to a new post in another school. All those involved with the induction and professional formation of this teacher should take satisfaction not only from her first promotion but also from her subsequent career. It reflects credit on the school.

- 'I look back on my spell in that school as time well spent.' When an employee retires it is important that he can be sure that his work has been valued. The retirement party and leaving present are an important part of this process. It may also be important for a senior manager or governor to attempt to put the individual's career in an appropriate, positive context. Individuals who have given many years to work deserve to be assured that this has been of value and importance, even if there have been differences of view or emphasis.

Students

Many schools will have a regular arrangement whereby students spend time in the school as part of their course. This may include school students on work experience and nursery nurse students and teachers on their period of initial teacher training (ITT). In recent years some schools have seen it as an undesirable and costly burden to take ITT students on placement and there has been debate over the level of remuneration from the higher education institutions benefiting from a Teacher Training Agency grant. While placements demand time and commitment, they can also bring considerable rewards in a time of difficult recruitment and through the energy, insight and enthusiasm the best trainees can bring, especially to an established staff. Proper arrangements need to be in place to ensure that all those coming into the school as students are inducted into the school's pattern of work and expectations. Equally, care needs to be taken to ensure that their needs are properly catered for so that their time in school is a good experience. The induction of students will need to include an introduction to the school's policies that will affect them. These will include policies about the care of pupils, health and safety issues and confidentiality. For child protection purposes, the school should satisfy itself that the necessary clearances have been obtained by the placing institution. If there is any doubt on this matter the school should insist on taking the appropriate action itself to obtain the necessary clearance. Most students commencing courses after September 2002 at colleges of higher education will have been checked by the college.

Volunteers

Many of the comments made about students will also apply to volunteers. Most, but not all, volunteers in the school are likely to be parents. For most volunteers the school will need to ensure that it has initiated the appropriate clearance checks. There will need to be a period of induction into the school for all volunteers, although for many parents this may be quite short and informal. If the volunteer is undertaking work for which they have no recent training, the issue of the provision of training for the task may arise. It is usually helpful to discuss with the volunteer the boundaries for their work, both in terms of what they will and will not do in the school and in terms of the period for which they will do it. If it has been clear from the start that the volunteer has agreed to offer two hours a week for a term, then towards the end of that term they can either be thanked for their contribution or a new agreement can be discussed for the following term. Some volunteers give many years of service to a school; others use volunteering at school as a way of re-entering the labour market after a period of caring for their children. Schools gain much benefit from both kinds of volunteer.

This chapter can only provide an introduction to the complex issues involved in the staffing of schools. It is a most important subject on which no one should feel inhibited from seeking advice from specialists in the diocesan or LEA office.

The National Society/Church House Publishing has published the following series of booklets on staffing issues, which develop in detail the themes touched on in this chapter.

Selecting, Appointing and Developing Staff in Church Schools – for employees in Voluntary Aided, Foundation and Voluntary Controlled Schools, Lankshear, David, 2001.

Managing Staff Sickness Absence – Procedures for employees in Voluntary Aided and Foundation Schools, 2000.

Discipline and Grievance Procedures – for employees in Voluntary Aided and Foundation Schools, 2000.

Redundancy Procedures – for employees in Voluntary Aided and Foundation Schools, 2000.

Capability Procedure – for employees in Voluntary Aided and Foundation Schools, 2000.

Churches Serving Schools (second edition), Lankshear, David, 2002.

Pocket Prayers for Teachers, Lankshear, David, 2002.

More details on all the issues raised in this chapter can be found on www.churchschools.co.uk.

Governors: a major responsibility

A strong, well-led governing body, supportive of the school, its teachers and its mission makes an important contribution to the school's well-being and effectiveness. The foundation governors will have an especial care for the school's Christian character.

The Way Ahead – paragraph 8.6

In the last 20 years there has been a huge growth in the role and importance of school governors. Being a governor no longer involves turning up to one meeting a term and occasionally for worship at harvest or Christmas. It is now a major piece of Christian and community service. No one should undertake the role lightly. It involves time, energy and a willingness to become involved in the life of the school on a regular basis over a significant period of time. Churches should recognize and support all those who undertake the responsibility of being a governor in a Church school.

New regulations following the Education Act 2002 will seek to refocus the respective duties of the governing body and of the headteacher, emphasizing the strategic role of the governing body and removing from it some detailed responsibilities. However, some of the detailed work governors have undertaken in the past has strategic impact, as over staff appointments. So the governing body's policy-making role will become even more important. If, for example, they are less practically involved in staff appointments than hitherto, they will need to make prior policy decisions about such matters as the level of Christian commitment to be expected of teachers who will be appointed in future years, where it is a voluntary aided school. The governing body's role in staff discipline will largely be reduced to one of hearing appeals, so this will require greater strategic clarity over matters of discipline and performance. The new regulations will also require changes to be implemented over the next few years to the constitution of the governing body in order to create greater flexibility.

In summary, the task of the governing body is to develop policy in consultation with the staff of the school, to approve the policies thus developed and to monitor the implementation of these policies as necessary. The headteacher, aided by the senior leadership and management team of the school, where this exists, is responsible for the implementation of these policies and the day-to-day management of the school.

The constitution of the governing body is laid down in the Instrument of Government. When the school has a religious character, this document also contains an 'ethos statement'. This statement is derived from the school's trust deed but lays out in modern language the main purposes of the school. All the policies that the governing body develops and approves for the school should take this statement as their starting point.

Membership of governing bodies

There are several ways of being appointed or elected to the governing body of a Church school. The exact constitution of the governing body, indicating how many governors are to be elected or appointed by the various routes and who in each case is the electing or appointing body, is laid down in the Instrument of Government and must comply with the legal requirements for the type and size of school. These will largely in future be expressed in proportions. There are detailed regulations about people who may not be governors of schools of any kind, for example, by virtue of their age or by having demonstrated that they cannot be trusted to run a business. The governing body is a body corporate made up of individuals together entrusted with the responsibility for making decisions about the expenditure of large amounts of money and making a significant impact on the lives of their employees, the pupils and the wider community. They must together and individually behave in a trustworthy manner.

Foundation governors

In Church schools this is the description of the governors appointed by the Church authorities. In an Anglican school it is usual for the incumbent of the parish, by virtue of office, to be a member of the governing body. This is called being an ex officio governor. In rare cases the incumbent may not be able to be a governor, for example, if there are more than two schools in the parish or benefice of which he or she is expected to be the ex officio governor. If this is the case he or she should contact the diocesan director of education, who will arrange for the archdeacon to nominate someone else from the Church to take on the duties. This is usually what happens if there is an interregnum (the period of time between vicars). Other foundation governors will mostly be active laypeople. The Instrument of Government will indicate which church organization has the responsibility for nominating the foundation governors. In Anglican schools it is common for there to be a mixture of nominating bodies, including the local Parochial Church Council and the Diocesan Board of Education. Some of the foundation governors must also be parents of pupils at the school at the time when they are nominated. The Instrument should make it clear who is responsible for ensuring that their nominees are parents. Most Diocesan Boards of Education have clear policies about the qualifications and characteristics of the people they are prepared to nominate as governors of the Church schools in the diocese. Where this is the case it is usually helpful if the other bodies who nominate foundation governors also have regard to this policy.

Teacher and staff governors

In every school there are arrangements for the teachers and staff employed at the school to elect one or more of their number to the governing body. Should a teacher or staff governor move to a post in another school they would cease to be a governor and a new election would be necessary.

The headteacher as a governor

The headteacher of the school may choose to be a member of the governing body. Most do so. Headteachers can change their minds about the decision at any time. If the headteacher decides not to be a member of the governing body he or she is still entitled to attend meetings of the governing body. Headteachers who are not members of the governing body can speak but cannot vote at governing body meetings.

Parent governors

The parents of the school are entitled to vote for one or more of their number to serve as governors of the school. Any parent who is elected must have a child attending the school when they take up office. If the child subsequently leaves, the parent may complete their full term of office, but may not stand for re-election. The governing body is well advised to delegate to the headteacher the conduct of an election for parent governor, including the sometimes difficult process of drawing up a register of electors, advice on which will be available from the LEA.

Parent governors from all schools in the LEA can elect one of their number to represent parents on the overview and scrutiny committees of the Local Authority that deal with matters affecting schools within the Authority.

Local Education Authority governor

The LEA nominates one or more governors to the school. The choice is a matter for the LEA. They are usually councillors or people active in the local community. They should be expected, like other governors, to play a full part in the school and actively to support the school as a Church school. They will naturally also represent the interests of the Local Authority, but they cannot be expected to speak or act on behalf of the Authority over matters that require advice or an interpretation of the Authority's judgement. It is important that the clerk to the governing body acts quickly to notify the LEA when a vacancy for such a governor occurs.

Minor Local Authority governor

In some schools, in some areas where there is a local council at a lower tier of local government than the Local Education Authority, the local council (referred to as the Minor Local Authority) is entitled to nominate a governor for co-option. In rural areas the MLA governor can be an important link between the school and the local civil parish, community or town.

Co-opted governors

Some categories of school (not voluntary aided schools) may have provision within their Instrument of Government for the governing body to co-opt governors. Such co-options may represent developing partnerships between the school and local businesses or may enable the governing body to bring in members with particular skills or experience.

Sponsorship governors

Where local partnerships are developed into a full sponsorship agreement, part of that formal sponsorship arrangement may include the creation of a place for one or more sponsorship governors. This will require the making of a new Instrument of Government and, in the case of a voluntary aided school, an increase in the number of foundation governors.

The chair of the governing body

At its first meeting of the academic year the governing body must elect or re-elect one of its number to the chair. Before the requirement for an annual election, the incumbent was automatically the chairperson in Church schools. Church school governing bodies should find the most appropriate member of the governing body to chair their meetings. The person who chairs the governing body must be someone who can conduct the meetings of the governing body inclusively and expeditiously and who has the commitment and can make the time to know and be known at the school. He or she must be able to lead the work of the governing body and to take public responsibility for that work on occasions such as the annual meeting for parents. It is also important to spend purposeful and suitably structured time with the headteacher.

Where the incumbent does not chair the governing body, he or she may feel more able to concentrate on the spiritual and pastoral duties of chaplaincy in the school. Many incumbents would see these as their prime responsibilities in a Church school; they are not, of course, incompatible with chairing the governing body.

Observers

Sometimes individuals may be invited to attend meetings of the governing body as observers. Such people may speak if invited to do so by the chair, but they may not vote. They must agree to be bound by the same rules of confidentiality and corporate responsibility as full members of the governing body.

The clerk to the governing body

The clerk to the governing body acts as secretary to the governors. He or she prepares the agenda for governing body meetings (in consultation with the chair and the headteacher), sends out notices of meetings and takes the minutes. In some cases clerks deal similarly with meetings of committees of the governing body although, for reasons of cost, alternative arrangements are sometimes made. Even where the LEA provides clerks as a service to the school, the school is (effectively, if not in fact) the employer of the clerk and must pay for the service. It may not be advisable for someone employed in the school for other purposes (e.g. the school secretary) to be the clerk, as this might lead to a perceived conflict of interest, but there is no reason in law why this should not be the case. It is no longer lawful under school government regulations for a member of the governing body to undertake the duties of clerk. The clerk will receive and deal with correspondence on behalf of the governing body. Some schools may retain distant memories of 'correspondents' but the old 'correspondent to the managers' in a primary school became clerk to the governing body in the education legislation of 1980. It is no longer appropriate for the governing body to have a member acting as correspondent.

The chief education officer (CEO) and the diocesan director of education (DDE)

The holders of both these offices, and their representatives, may attend the meetings of the governing body under certain circumstances. The reason for this is to enable the governors to draw on the advice available from these two offices. Their rights of attendance were enshrined in successive acts of primary legislation including the School Standards and Framework Act 1998 but, following the Education Act 2002, these will be provided in regulations. It is important that the clerk ensure routinely that both the CEO and the DDE receive proper notice of all the meetings, a copy of the agenda, the minutes and any other papers that are being presented at the meeting.

Committees

The governing body may appoint committees to undertake some of its work, although there are certain decisions that cannot be delegated. Two obvious examples of such committees are the admissions committee that makes decisions about which children to admit to the school in voluntary aided or foundation schools and the staffing committee. Some of the committees will meet regularly and form a permanent part of the work of the governors. Others will take the nature of informal working parties set up to undertake a particular task and ending their work when that task is complete. It is important that the governing body gives any committee or task group that it creates a clear brief in writing, so that there is no potential for misunderstanding. This will state whether the committee has deliberative, advisory or decision-making powers and, if the latter, the limits on those powers. The full governing body should not debate again issues that it has delegated to committees, unless the committee requests further guidance on policy issues. It is not necessary for every member of a committee to be a full member of the governing body.

The governors' responsibilities

All members of the governing body have similar responsibilities.

- They are responsible for the overall policies of the school and for ensuring that the headteacher runs the school in accordance with those policies.

- They are responsible for representing the interests of the group that elects or nominates them on the governing body.

The foundation governors are, therefore, particularly responsible for ensuring that a Church school is organized in accordance with the traditions and practices of the Church.

- They are responsible for ensuring that the needs of the school are represented appropriately to the body that nominated or elected them.

It will be clear that the governors are not there to manage the school on a day-to-day basis. That is the task of the headteacher.

The governors also have a duty to elect a chair and vice-chair each year, to conduct their business efficiently and fairly and to ensure that any funds entrusted to them are administered properly.

The governing body of the school has a responsibility for the development and approval of all the key policies within which the school functions. A prime task of governors is, therefore, to take an active part in the development of these policies. In this the governors will be working closely with the teaching staff of the school, and, for certain topics, other school staff as well.

It is often helpful for governors to take a special responsibility for an area of the curriculum or of the school's work. In doing this they are undertaking to develop a good working relationship with the subject coordinator or head of department. Where a new policy document is being developed in an area, the teacher responsible will probably prepare the draft and discuss it with the headteacher and the governor with that area of responsibility. When it is ready for presentation to the whole governing body the three key contributors, the teacher, the head and the governor, will agree how the document is to be presented and who will make the presentation. Should questions be asked at the Annual Parents' Meeting about a specialist area it would be normal for the governor who takes an interest in that area to answer, with the headteacher providing any further depth that the questions require. One of the governors must take on the role of governor for Special Educational Needs, another for child protection and another for issues arising from appraisal of staff.

An important duty of governors is contributing to the network of communication, without which no school can function. While all governors contribute to all aspects of this there is a special expectation that governors will support and assist in the communication between the school and the body or group who nominated them.

Governors also have duties in the appointment of staff. These have been dealt with in some detail in the chapter on staff issues, but the principles are worth rehearsing here. The governors have direct responsibility (in voluntary aided and foundation schools) or responsibility delegated from the LEA (in voluntary controlled schools) for the appointment of the staff to the school. Much of the detailed work will be delegated to the headteacher and others in a clearly defined manner. Being responsible for appointing the staff also implies accepting responsibility for their support, encouragement and professional development. It also implies accepting the responsibility for taking action if things have gone wrong. It is not adequate to argue that 'I wasn't a governor when Mrs Smith was appointed, so it is nothing to do with me'. Governors have a corporate responsibility and, therefore, becoming a member of the governing body implies taking on the responsibility for previous decisions and policies.

It seems impossible not to mention money. School budgets loom very large in the running of a school. The governing body is responsible for setting the school budget and monitoring its expenditure. The precise way in which these responsibilities are exercised will vary between different LEAs and will reflect their schemes for the Fair funding of schools. The governing body also has responsibility for other funds than those delegated to them by the LEA. These may include the school 'voluntary fund', trust money held for the school or funds to pay for developments in the school building. All funds should be managed with openness and honesty and in accordance with good accounting practice. The National Society has developed a booklet of guidance on the management of charitable funds, about which those governors involved in financial matters should know.

Conduct of meetings

The chair of the governing body, the clerk and the headteacher will have discussed the agenda in good time before the meeting to ensure that it is well prepared. Preparation will include ensuring that the papers go out in good time before the meeting, so that all members of the governing body are able to consider the issues and prepare themselves for the discussion. The papers should also reach any adviser for the same reasons. There need to be special arrangements, known to all governors, in the rare cases where urgent business that needs to be dealt with at a meeting arises after the agenda has been prepared. 'Any other business' must not be used for a member of the governing body to bring up an item that should really be discussed only after preparation, or that is the business of a committee. This is particularly important in controversy or where there are criticisms of a member of staff or of another member of the governing body. It is often helpful to restrict items of this kind through a notice on the agenda requiring 48 hours' notice to be given to the chair of the intention to raise an item. Some items will appear regularly on every agenda, some will appear on an annual cycle and others only when they are needed. Some of the regular items include:

Prayer

Meetings of a Church school governing body should normally start with prayer. This will help to focus the meeting and remind all present that they are involved in work being done in the name of God. If there are individual members of the governing body who do not feel able to be present during prayers, arrangements should be made for them to join the meeting after the prayers have been said. It is important that the agenda makes it clear when the prayers will happen.

Election of chair and vice-chair

This is an annual item, taken at the first meeting of the school year. In some years it will probably be no more than a formality; at other times it will be one of the most important decisions a governing body can make. The person best able to fulfil either of these two roles should be elected to the chair (see above).

Headteacher's report

This item will appear on the agenda of every meeting. The headteacher should present a written report, normally circulated with the agenda, and be prepared to answer questions on it. It is helpful if governors ask for items that they would like to see included in this report, as it will avoid the report falling into a routine pattern. It should not be used as a means of raising items of substance that should have been on the main agenda. Where there are decisions to be taken by the governing body, it is helpful if these appear as separate items, so that it is clear what is required. The report should be a report, not a separate mini agenda.

Action Plans

Following an inspection, either by OFSTED (ESTYN in Wales) under section 10 of the School Inspection Act 1996 or a denominational inspection under section 23, the governing body must develop an Action Plan. Once the governing body has approved it, it should receive regular reports on its implementation, so that governors can be sure that the school is making a full response to the key issues raised in the inspection. The governing body must report to parents on its Action Plan. Governors should be aware that inspectors will always look for evidence of the implementation of previous action plans when they inspect the school. Failure to implement an Action Plan is taken as clear evidence of serious weaknesses in the governance or management of the school.

Education Development Plans (EDPs)/Education Strategic Plans (ESPs)

Every LEA must produce an Education Development Plan (Education Strategic Plan in Wales) in consultation with local schools. These cover a three-year period but there are provisions for an annual review. Within the plan there must be targets agreed with each school for the educational attainment of its pupils. The EDP/ESP will therefore be a regular item on the governing body agenda as the governors will need to know not only the content of the plan as it refers to their school but also the action that is being taken to achieve the targets that have been set.

Asset management plans (AMP)

Every LEA must have an asset management plan. This is discussed in detail on pages 111–12. The AMP and work related to it will be a regular feature of governing body's agendas.

Other items for the agenda

Items on admissions, finance, buildings, Special Educational Needs, staffing and the curriculum will all be regular features of the agenda, but they have all been covered in some detail in other sections of the book.

The focus of this section has, so far, been on the formal structure of the meetings. This is because the meetings of the governing

83

body are formal affairs and must be conducted properly. The business of the governors must be carried through effectively. There are other issues, however.

The formality of the meeting should not detract from the quality of the relations that should exist between members of the governing body. In the chapters on parents and children much emphasis was placed on the quality of relations and the theological ideas that should inform them. Two groups of adults, the staff and the governors, are responsible for creating and maintaining these relations. If relations between members of these two groups do not demonstrate the principles that the school is seeking to promote, little of lasting value will be achieved.

All governors, not just the chair, must ensure that every member of the governing body is encouraged to voice his or her opinion in an appropriate fashion, to contribute to debate and to have their views acknowledged. This does not mean that the only way forward is total consensus. Nor does it give every individual a veto. It does mean that, on important or controversial issues, the chair should ensure that governors have ample opportunity to make their points. Having debated the issues and come to an agreement about them, all members of the governing body should then accept the decisions of the majority and support them in public. This should be the case even where a member has been unable to attend a particular meeting.

Confidentiality

The details of the discussions in a governing body should remain confidential. Governors must know that what they say during a meeting will not be repeated outside it. If governors are to have confidence in each other they have to know that everyone present is observing these basic rules for committee work. The minutes will record the decisions that have been taken. They should not record the detailed discussion. Minutes of the governing body are not themselves confidential and can be seen by anyone interested once they have been approved. Items that the governing body decides to retain in confidence should be recorded and kept separately. The decision about which, if any, items should be kept confidential can be made when the agenda is prepared or at the end of a meeting of the governing body. It is good practice following governing body meetings for members of staff to be given information about any important decisions. It is not, however, necessary for members of staff routinely to receive copies of minutes.

School policies

The governing body must approve a range of policies on which the school will depend for its good management. Some of these are required by law. Others, although not statutory, are so important that inspectors and others concerned with the school's performance will ask to see them. Governors should not approve a policy that they do not understand; it is, therefore, important that governors read draft policies carefully, hear presentations on them from appropriate teaching or other staff and ask any questions that they may have before giving their approval. Once approved by the governing body, the policy should be supported by all governors, who should also be satisfied that measures are in place to ensure that the policy is being implemented appropriately in the school.

First among these policies is the ethos statement that forms part of the Instrument of Government. From this statement the governors will have derived a mission statement or set of aims for the school. All other policies should relate to these basic statements of the purpose of the school. The policies, which the governors should consider for approval, will cover all the major areas of the curriculum, not just the national curriculum but RE, school worship and the extra curriculum, and large numbers of other matters such as staffing, pay for staff, the delegation of financial responsibility, school security, pupil behaviour, how to deal with complaints and the school's communication of itself to its wider community.

Within every school there should be a scheduled process of policy review in order to ensure that no policy becomes out of date or ignored because it has not been discussed for a number of years. New staff and governors should be made aware of the key school policies as part of their induction programme.

Visiting the school

All governors should seek to visit the school, after due consultation with the headteacher, sufficiently regularly to be confident that they know something of its work. Some governors, because they fulfil other roles in the life of the school, visit quite regularly and may make a significant contribution in these other capacities. Governors should discuss plans for school visiting at least once a year as part of their agenda, in order to ensure that these visits are coordinated and do not become a burden to the school. The purpose of the visit is not to inspect or to monitor an aspect of the school. For these matters the governors must rely on the professional service of those they employ and of those who support the school, even where they can themselves bring a professional interest to bear. It is good practice at the end of a visit for a governor to discuss what they have seen with the headteacher or other senior member of staff in order to ensure that they have understood the context of their observations.

Training for governors

When a governor is first appointed to a school there should be a period of induction to enable him or her to take a full and informed part in the work of the governing body as quickly as possible. This may include:

1. being given a folder of the key policies, documents and papers, including the Instrument of Government, recent inspection reports, and others relating to the work of the governing body;

2. making an informal visit to the school;

3. meeting the headteacher;

4. meeting the chair of the governors;

5. being given a mentor from amongst the experienced governors.

Other training activities for governors take two basic forms:

1. being part of a training activity organized for the whole governing body of the school;

2. going on a course or conference as a representative of the governing body or from personal interest.

Over a period of time every governor will be involved in both types of training activity.

The main providers of training for governors are the LEA, the diocese and the associations of governors. These are also the main sources of advice to governors outside the staff of the school. Some governors may be interested in relating the training that they undertake to other forms of professional or personal development in which they are engaged. It is possible to find courses being offered to governors that have a clear relationship to validated programmes of study, leading to higher education qualifications in some areas. Your diocese or LEA will be able to provide details of these.

Within the school budget, or from other funds available to the school, governors should ensure that there is some funding available for their participation in training. Governors give up much free time to the service of the school. They should not also be expected to pay for their training out of their own pockets.

Finance

There are two distinct areas of finance for which the governing body has responsibility. Each of the areas has its own rules and requires a particular type of response from the governing body.

Fair funding (LMS): delegated funds

The Local Education Authority delegates funds to schools to cover the costs of paying the staff and day-to-day running. Each local authority has its own scheme, with accompanying regulations on how the scheme is to operate in practice. These schemes must conform to guidelines laid down by the Department for Education and Skills or (in Wales) the National Assembly. These bodies must also approve the schemes. The Local Education Authority must consult schools locally about these schemes. Under new legislation this will be done through the work of the local Schools Forum. Governors have to develop policies on expenditure, such as staff pay policy, and see that these are implemented. They should approve the annual budget and some governors may be involved in its development. The governing body must also satisfy itself that the budget is being managed efficiently in line with the policy or guidelines that it has approved. It must also ensure that all areas of expenditure to be covered by the budget are properly identified. Where reserves are being built up against future large-scale expenditure, governors must ensure that these are being properly managed and that the reserves are only sufficiently large to cover the planned expenditure. Where they are asked to approve savings or cuts in planned expenditure they should be aware of the implications of these cuts or delays in spending on the future welfare of the school.

Governing body funds

In voluntary aided and foundation schools in particular, it is likely that the governing body will have some funds in its control other than those delegated by the LEA. These funds may be the result of building appeals or the proceeds of letting the school buildings to third parties. Some governing bodies also benefit from trusts held in the name of the school. Charitable funds fall under the regime created by the Charities Acts. Detailed advice on the management of these funds is available in a National Society booklet *Church Schools and Charity Law*. The important principle to establish at this stage is that it is essential for the various funds to be kept separate and for movements between them to be carefully recorded. The governing body has absolute responsibility for the money entrusted by the parents and supporters of the school and must be prepared to account for the use of the money to anyone with a legitimate interest.

External relations

There is a wide range of groups within the local community and beyond with which the governing body of a Church school should maintain close working relations. Many of these groups will appoint members to the governing body and those governors will naturally ensure that there are good channels of communication between the school and the body that appointed them. Locally, the principal groups will be the parents, the parish or parishes served by the school and the wider local community. The school's prospectus of information and any newsletter that the school publishes will be two of the ways in which communication is taken forward. How people are greeted when they visit the school or telephone the school office, and their perception of how they are spoken to by the headteacher and the staff of the school will be very important.

Relationships with the Local Education Authority and the Diocesan Board of Education will be of a different nature. There will be a close professional relationship between the staff of the Local Education Authority, the Diocesan Board of Education and those who work most closely with them in the school. As always in a school, much will depend on the headteacher, but the chair of the governing body and those responsible for the school premises and finance will also have an important role in maintaining good relationships. The headteacher and those members of staff with curriculum responsibilities will know the advisory staff of the Local Authority and the Diocesan Board. The school secretary should maintain a list of the names and contact numbers of those within the Local Education Authority and the Diocesan Board of Education staff who are most often in contact with the school.

From time to time the school will come into contact with the local press, radio or television. This will often be because the school has some good news that it wishes to share or an event that it wishes to publicize. It is often helpful to have a member of staff or one of the governing body who maintains these links with the local media on behalf of the school, through whom such reports can be channelled. This will help to develop a good working relationship with local reporters, so that they know whom to contact if they wish to discuss a school event or follow up a story. It also helps other staff and governors to know that there is a colleague who will answer questions on behalf of the school, so that they do not feel pressured into doing so. Indeed, if there is an event that needs delicate handling it is essential that only those who have been given authority to do so by the governing body speak to the press on behalf of the school. In sensitive situations help should be sought from the media relations team of the Local Education Authority or the diocesan communications officer.

Management

Governors have a key role in the development of policy in the school and the appointment of the staff who will be responsible for the day-to-day management of the school. It is not the governors' task to manage the school. They can facilitate good management in the school by providing clear policies and being supportive of the headteacher and the school leadership team. Governors do have one important shared management task, however, which is to manage their own business and meetings effectively.

This chapter has outlined some of the main duties of the governing body. Being a member of a school governing body can be a daunting task but it is also a great privilege. Governors accept responsibility for everything that happens within a school, and are charged with ensuring that every pupil receives the best possible education.

The National Society/Church House Publishing has published *Church Schools and Charity Law*, 2000.

More details of all the issues raised in this chapter can be found on www.churchschools.co.uk.

Curriculum issues

> We warmly welcome the work of those engaged in developing
> methodologies for a distinctively Christian approach to the curriculum
> and materials for the theory and practice of Christian education. We
> also welcome the developmental work that has been taking place in a
> number of schools to give expression to their chosen ethos statements
> through class work and in so doing to engage in the spiritual, moral,
> social and cultural development of pupils ...
>
> *The Way Ahead*, paragraph 4.11

Schools are about the education of children. Therefore, what is
learned in schools is of vital importance to those who are charged
with the management and governance of schools. This learning
comes in two interrelated forms. First, there is the formal curriculum of the school, much of it set in a framework of legal
requirements and national or local guidance. Secondly, there is
what children and young people learn as a result of being part of
the school community, participating in its life, rituals and pattern
of relationships for several years. This second area is more often
left to chance than the first and is less well defined. This chapter
will explore some of the issues that are raised for Church schools
by both types of learning. Every Church school must have an ethos
statement as part of its Instrument of Government. This statement
should sum up in a few words the basis on which the school was
founded and on which the whole of the curriculum, in both of the
senses used above, will be built. All ethos statements in Anglican
schools should make clear that the school's life draws deeply on
Anglican tradition and teaching.

The formal curriculum

Since 1988 the main content of the formal curriculum has been enshrined in law. The Education Reform Act of that year introduced two key curriculum concepts, the basic curriculum and the national curriculum.

The basic curriculum is defined as religious education and those subjects that form the national curriculum. Every school in the maintained system must provide at least the basic curriculum for pupils of statutory school age. This is pupils' entitlement, although greater provision for disapplication and variation of the curriculum is currently being introduced post-14.

The national curriculum is defined as a particular set of ten subjects (eleven in Wales), whose content is laid down in syllabuses drawn up for the Government by the Qualifications and Curriculum Authority (ACCAC in Wales). The syllabuses for all the subjects are created externally to the school, except in some very limited cases. Governors and teachers working on reviews of school curriculum policies must, therefore, ensure that they know what the current syllabuses contain, and seek to ensure that, as far as possible, their own documentation reflects that content.

Religious education

The source of the syllabus for religious education varies according to the category of the school. Community schools and others that do not have a religious character must follow the locally agreed syllabus published by the Local Authority. For voluntary aided schools with a religious character the RE syllabus is a matter for the governing body and is expected to reflect the particular traditions and beliefs of the denomination of the school. In Church of England schools the governing body should follow the advice of the diocese, which may provide a Diocesan Syllabus or curriculum guidance supplementary to the locally agreed syllabus. In Wales the Church in Wales published a Provincial Syllabus for religious education in 2002. If there is no external guidance, governors in such schools have to take the full responsibility for ensuring that their syllabus for religious education fully reflects the traditions of their faith. In voluntary controlled or foundation schools religious education must be provided, in accordance with the religious character of the school, where individual parents request it for their own children. In such circumstances it can be provided by reserved teachers (see p. 49). For all other children the syllabus is that produced under the auspices of the Local Authority (the agreed syllabus). Every LEA has a current syllabus for religious education, which has been developed or approved by the Local Authority's Agreed Syllabus Conference (ASC). Support for the Local Authority syllabus is focused through the local Standing Advisory Council for Religious Education (SACRE). In all schools parents have the right to withdraw their children from religious education lessons in whole or in part.

At the time of writing there is considerable interest in the possible production of a national framework for religious education. This would be designed as a resource for local Conferences in their work to produce a locally agreed syllabus. The publication of such a framework by the Qualifications and Curriculum Authority would supplement the nationally produced Schemes of Work for RE and, like them, would undoubtedly have wide significance for the subject. Such a framework would, for example, greatly assist those responsible for the training of RE teachers. It would not, however, replace the need for active local support for RE in all schools in which the Church of England has a particular role, forming as it does a single committee on the ASC and SACRE, without whose agreement no new syllabus can be approved.

The national curriculum

In the period since it was first introduced, the national curriculum has engendered great changes in schools and been the engine, not without controversy, for considerable improvements in standards of education. Before 1988 only RE was compulsory and every other aspect of the school curriculum was a matter for the professionals in the school, with the advice of the LEA and, remotely, of the Schools' Council. There were great debates about how far the curriculum should be prescriptive and early mistakes were made. Since those days the curriculum has undergone two major reviews and been subject to a great many detailed changes. It has more recently been supplemented by the literacy and numeracy initiatives that have affected the way in which primary schools in particular approach these aspects of education. Further developments in the national curriculum content have come about with the introduction of citizenship and the concern to provide a more varied and flexible approach to the public examination system so that it better reflects the wide range of talents, interests and needs of pupils between the ages of 14 and 19.

Many of the early controversies around the national curriculum seem long past. Teachers accept the need for the curriculum itself and for rigorous assessment of the progress of their pupils, at least for diagnostic purposes. A contentious issue that remains is the degree to which prescription undermines the professionalism of teachers. But the national curriculum itself does not prescribe the manner in which it is taught. Moreover it is supposed to take only 70 per cent of total teaching time. If this can be achieved there is space to provide the suggested 5 per cent of curriculum time for religious education (though many religious schools manage a higher percentage) and also to have some material that is not in the prescribed curriculum, but which reflects the needs of the pupils.

Personal, social and health education (PSHE)

This is one example of a curriculum topic for which some space needs to be found within the teaching time available in a school. Discussion continues among educationalists about whether this topic is a curriculum subject in its own right or whether it is actually a cross-curricular issue drawing on contributions from most subject areas. It is probable that if, within this umbrella topic, aspects of health education, sex education, careers education, parenting, drugs education, citizenship, safety and relationships are all to find an appropriate slot, then it will need to have a specific allocation of teaching time. Many of the elements within PSHE are of particular significance in a Church school. Governors will wish to ensure that approaches adopted are informed by Christian insights and reflect the ethos statement of the school.

Sex and relationships education

Sex education must appear as part of the curriculum in secondary schools. Governors of primary schools may decide whether the school should make provision for sex education. If they decide that the school should not provide formal teaching on this subject they should provide their staff with clear guidance on how children's questions about it are answered. Parents have the right to withdraw their children from all aspects of sex education that are not required by the national curriculum. Education about relationships will be present in every school as part of what is learned from being part of the school community. There will now be some formal teaching in this area as well, either as part of sex and relationships education, PSHE or in other subject areas. Teaching about relationships must include some teaching about marriage. It is a requirement of the law that pupils 'learn the nature of marriage and its importance for family life and the bringing up of children'. The National Society has produced a web resource to help teachers and governors explore how the teaching of marriage may be integrated within the curriculum as a whole. This resource has been designed as a contribution to curriculum development in all schools. Church schools will need to reflect on how much additional information they will need to include in order to reflect properly the Christian understanding of marriage.

The hidden curriculum

Spiritual, moral, social and cultural education (SMSC)

The inspection regime introduced following the 1992 Act established the high importance of schools' responsibility for the spiritual, moral, social and cultural development of their pupils. Teachers have become increasingly confident in handling these four crucial aspects of the underlying curriculum or 'hidden curriculum' as it has sometimes been known. This is a term that is sometimes used to describe those informal aspects of learning that occur simply because pupils are part of a school community. They learn about relationships principally, not by being taught or by discussing, but by experiencing the quality of relationships that exist within the school and within their home. They learn about values in the same way. They learn about the benefits of being good and the problems that are caused when you are bad, through experience and observation within the community. This is powerful learning. It is learning from every adult involved in the school and from each other. It is very important that the adults who are responsible for the governance and management of the school understand the need to develop clear policies in these areas and to take action to ensure that they are followed.

Much could be said about each of these areas. Schools are generally confident in dealing with the moral and social development of pupils. For Anglican schools, spiritual development should be an area of considerable strength and should reflect the Anglican character of the school (see pp. 3–5). Cultural development has taken on fresh meaning and importance since the events of the summer of 2001. The demand for education to promote community cohesion and social inclusion within multicultural British society should encourage Anglican schools to look afresh at their policies for cultural development. The Government and Parliament have resisted the calls from a few politicians and commentators that would require 'faith schools' to have specific quotas of pupils from other faiths or cultures, although the Church has committed itself to Anglican schools' being inclusive as well as distinctive. But the cultural development of pupils within any school community will be promoted as they grow in understanding of other faiths and cultures. This can be advanced through effective twinning arrangements between schools that reflect different cultures. These should not be patronizing and they should promote sympathetic understanding through a genuine desire to learn from, as well as about, others. There is also an important opportunity for Anglican schools, as part of the worldwide Anglican Communion in which Christianity finds expression in a host of profoundly different cultures, to learn from and about those various cultures. The Web makes this possible now as never before.

The 'hidden curriculum' should not be hidden from teachers and governors. The National Society has published a series of booklets on these topics, which deal with issues in great detail. Every Church school should have copies of these booklets available and should have incorporated some of their insights into the school's policy documents. In 2001 the Society published material for staff development in spiritual education in a booklet entitled *Feeding Minds and Touching Hearts*.

School worship

Every pupil in the school must take part in an act of collective worship every school day unless their parents have exercised their legal right to withdraw them from worship. This worship may involve the whole school, a year group, a tutor group or class or any other grouping that the school would normally use to bring pupils together. The programme of worship in the school will make a significant contribution to the ethos of the school, the hidden curriculum and the spiritual, moral, social and cultural development of the children in the school. The policy on which the programme of worship will be built will be based on the richness and diversity of the Anglican tradition of worship, while paying proper attention to the traditions of the local parish and the age and maturity of the children. Worship in a Church school will receive considerable attention in terms of provision of resources, planning and training opportunities for the staff involved in its management and leadership.

In a voluntary aided school, all teachers can and should be expected to attend and to take an appropriate part in the daily act of collective worship. Nothing should be organized that prevents any teacher or pupil taking part in the daily worship, which is at the very heart of school life. In voluntary controlled and foundation Anglican schools, the expectation of teachers is not the same but the school must provide Anglican daily worship for all pupils. In this the head will inevitably have a leading role. It is worth stating the point that the law on daily worship that applies to schools without a religious character, that it should be 'wholly or mainly of a broadly Christian character' taken over the term as a whole, does not apply to Anglican schools, in which the law expects the daily worship to reflect Anglican beliefs and traditions of worship. Since 1998 it has been possible for the daily requirement to be fulfilled for voluntary controlled and foundation schools, as well as for voluntary aided schools, by an act of worship in church. Increasing numbers of schools, primary as well as secondary, now celebrate the Eucharist sometimes in school or sometimes in church after careful preparation on a regular basis. Some are, once again, with the support of their parents, preparing children for baptism, for Holy Communion and/or for confirmation. These developments should be welcomed, encouraged and supported by the local church community. School worship, to which parents and the local community are invited and welcomed on a regular basis, is genuinely part of the worshipping life of the local church and should be seen as such. It can provide an excellent introduction to worship for those who might find attendance on Sunday in the parish church at first daunting or unfamiliar.

The National Society has published a wide range of material in support of school worship. Some of this is available in book form and some is available through the Society's web site.

Inspection

In Church schools there are two distinct elements to inspection. A jargon has grown up to distinguish them, which is derived from the sections of the Schools Inspection Act 1996, which defines them. Section 10 inspections are undertaken by teams appointed by OFSTED (ESTYN in Wales). These inspections cover all the aspects of a Church school that would be inspected in a community school but that are not inspected under section 23 inspections. A team led by a registered inspector carries out the section 10 inspections. They follow the pattern for inspection laid out in the relevant phase handbook published by OFSTED or ESTYN. Under section 23 of the Act the school governors appoint an inspector to inspect those aspects of the school that are conducted in accordance with the school's trust deed (for more detail see below). The National Society has created a training scheme for these inspectors and over 90 per cent of all section 23 inspections in Anglican schools are conducted by inspectors who have undergone this training. Both inspections should normally be carried out in the same academic year. In both cases the inspection report, which is a public document, is addressed to the governing body. The governing body must respond to each report by producing an Action Plan and ensuring that the plan is carried out.

Section 23 inspections apply to all schools that have a religious character, but affect the various categories of school within this group differently. The following table shows how each category of school will normally be affected.

	Voluntary aided	Voluntary controlled	Foundation
Religious education	Section 23	Section 10 (unless denominational religious education is provided, when that provision is inspected under section 23)	Section 10 (unless denominational religious education is provided, when that provision is inspected under section 23)
School worship	Section 23	Section 23	Section 23
Spiritual, moral, social and cultural education	Section 23 and section 10	Section 23 (if the governors ask for it) and section 10	Section 23 (if the governors ask for it) and section 10

Note: Section 10 inspectors will report on whether the school is complying with the law on school worship.

Every Anglican school should have a copy of the *Handbook on Inspection under Section 23* published by the National Society, as this provides clear and detailed guidance on what to expect from a section 23 inspection in an Anglican school.

Process of inspection

The inspection process is a very important one in the life of every school and has been responsible for improvements in the education offered in many schools. It is also a time when all the staff of the school feel themselves to be under considerable pressure. Therefore, the process must be well managed, and governors have an important part to play in this.

Parents are significantly involved, both in the pre-inspection meetings with the registered inspector and (in some cases) the section 23 inspector, and in the post-inspection meetings. Indeed, the Annual Parents' Meeting should receive reports on the implementation of the governing body's action plans following every inspection.

Pupils are also involved. They are, of course, part of the classes or groups being inspected. Some may be invited to provide comments to the inspectors or be interviewed by them. All, therefore, will be aware of the events of the inspection and the pressure on the staff; many will feel a pressure to 'perform' well so that their school will get a good report.

Whether schools have a 'short' or 'standard' inspection under section 10, they will all have the same basic pattern of inspection under section 23. The two reports, once they have been formally received, must involve a response from the school that is focused through the governors' Action Plan. The reports themselves are public documents and copies must be sent to all the bodies that nominate members of the governing body. Every parent should receive copies of the summaries of the reports and may have the full report if they request it.

It is important that the school manages the inspection process well, and that the governors maintain a positive view of the potential for the inspection to contribute to the future development of the school. They should also seek to ensure that the reports are read and understood in a balanced way so that what is good is celebrated and what needs attention is worked on.

Parental concerns and complaints

Sometimes parents become concerned about an aspect of the teaching or the content of the curriculum. In the first instance they should discuss their concerns with the class teacher or head of department. If they are not satisfied with the discussion then they should discuss the issue with the headteacher. Most issues are resolved at this stage. Occasionally the parent wishes to take the matter further. Every school will have a curriculum complaints procedure and the steps laid down in that procedure should then be followed.

Teaching methods

So far in this chapter little has been said about teaching methodology. The emphasis has been on curriculum policy, content and inspections. This is because methodology is almost entirely a matter of professional judgement for the teaching staff of the school. Issues of methodology will arise in the governing body in response to inspection or to requests for significant expenditure on buildings or equipment to enable improved teaching strategies to be adopted. Naturally governors will be interested in how pupils are taught, but they should expect to learn about this area as much through their school visits and their informal discussions with staff as through the business items on the governing body agenda. If pupils are to receive a good education in the school, governors will need to ensure that they give time and energy to discussion of curriculum issues.

The National Society/Church House Publishing has published:

Spiritual Development in Schools, Brown, Alan and Furlong, Jean, 1996

Social Development, Day, Pauline, 1997

Moral Education, Ainsworth, Janina and Brown, Alan, 1995

Cultural Development, Bailey, John, 1997

Feeding Minds and Touching Hearts, Brown, Alan and Seaman, Alison, 2001

Worship! Bailey, John, 1999

Teaching Christianity at Key Stage 1, Seaman, Alison and Owen, Graham, 1999

Teaching Christianity at Key Stage 2, Weatherley, Lillian and Reader, Trevor, 2001

and on the web site:

Teaching about Marriage

Valuing Cultural Diversity.

More details of all the issues raised in this chapter can be found on www.churchschools.co.uk.

The schools themselves

Voluntary Controlled and Voluntary Aided schools should rank equally in the care of the Church, and the Church should respond to schools in each category according to their needs.

The Way Ahead, paragraph 4.18

Categories of school

There are three types of maintained Church school, each with its own characteristics. There are some features that all Church schools share, which distinguish them from schools that do not have a religious foundation. In all Anglican schools:

- the school worship must relate to the Anglican tradition;

- trustees will own the school buildings (with very rare exceptions);

- governors control the use of the school premises outside school hours but there are some rights for the LEA (in voluntary controlled schools the foundation governors control the use of premises on a Sunday);

- there must be staff able to teach religious education in accordance with an Anglican syllabus;

- anyone appointed to be headteacher must be able to demonstrate, at least, their fitness and ability to preserve and develop the Anglican character of the school;

- The 'trust deed' aspects of the school's work are inspected under section 23 of the Act.

In all these areas diocesan directors of education will be able to provide advice to governing bodies.

The strange choice of the words 'voluntary aided' and 'voluntary controlled' to describe the main categories of Church school in the Education Act 1944 has led to some confusion over the years.

- Voluntary aided Church of England/Church in Wales school does not mean a school aided by the Church, but one owned and managed by the Church and aided by the LEA (and the DfES or Welsh National Assembly).

- Voluntary controlled Church of England/Church in Wales school does not mean a school controlled by the Church of England/Church in Wales. Though the LEA used to control these schools, now no single group of governors has control.

Two similar potential sources of confusion arose in September 1999 as a result of the School Standards and Framework Act.

- The first is between 'foundation schools' and 'foundation governors'. In all Church schools there are foundation governors, who are nominated by various Church bodies. Anglican Church schools are owned by trustees, who do not necessarily appoint governors directly. In foundation schools without a religious character the governing body owns the school site. There are partnership governors instead of foundation governors for these schools.

- The second potential confusion is between schools of any category that deliberately set out to make their facilities available to the local community and the category of schools known as 'community schools'. The name of this latter group of schools is designed to indicate that they are owned by the Local Education Authority and managed by governors representing the local community. It does not indicate that they are necessarily any more committed to serving their local community than schools of any other category.

In addition to the three categories of LEA maintained school mentioned above, recent Education Acts have created and

106

developed the concept of Academies. These are, in theory, independent schools that operate in the maintained sector under an agreement made directly with the Secretary of State, who provides their funding. Some Academies will be founded by dioceses and others and will have a Church religious character. A discussion of Academies is beyond the scope of this book.

The following tables summarize the differences between the three different types of Church school.

	Voluntary aided schools	Voluntary controlled schools	Foundation schools
Staff a) Teaching	Employed by the governors, the LEA usually, but not always, provides payroll services. Governors may seek evidence of Christian commitment from applications for teaching posts.	Appointed by governors, employed and paid by LEA. Governors are bound by LEA appointing policies. Governors should satisfy themselves that a candidate for the post of headteacher is suitable to support and develop the ethos of a voluntary controlled school.	Employed by the governors, paid by the LEA. Governors will be able to select teachers within the LEA policy. Governors should satisfy themselves that a candidate for the post of headteacher is suitable to support and develop the ethos of a foundation school.
Staff b) Support	Employed either by governors or contractors. If by governors, then paid by LEA.	Employed either by LEA or contractor. LEA employees usually appointed by the governors.	Employed either by governors or contractors. If by governors, then paid by LEA.

Worship	Reflects the Anglican tradition and can include worship in the parish church.	Reflects the Anglican tradition and can include worship in the parish church.	Reflects the Anglican tradition and can include worship in the parish church.
RE	Governors determine a syllabus that reflects the Anglican traditions. They should make use of the diocesan syllabus where this exists.	Local Authority agreed syllabus except for children whose parents have requested reserved teaching. The foundation governors have rights in the appointment of staff (called reserved teachers) to teach denominational religious education.	Local Authority agreed syllabus except for children whose parents have requested reserved teaching. The foundation governors have rights in the appointment of staff (called reserved teachers) to teach denominational religious education.
Membership of the governing body	Church (foundation) governors have an absolute majority over all other governors. The parish priest is usually ex officio a member of the governing body. The chair is elected by the governing body, on an annual basis. A proportion of foundation governors must also be parents.	Church (foundation) governors are in a minority. The parish priest is usually ex officio a member of the governing body. The chair is elected by the governing body, on an annual basis.	Church (foundation) governors are in a minority. The parish priest is usually ex officio a member of the governing body. The chair is elected by the governing body, on an annual basis.

Funding	LEA Fair funding formula. Governors' costs for building work from locally raised funds, PCC, local trusts and, usually, from trusts administered by the diocese.	LEA Fair funding formula.	LEA Fair funding formula.
Admissions	Governors determine the policy after consultation with the LEA and other admission authorities. They make the decision on which pupils to admit. The LEA has a role in the coordination of admissions procedures.	The LEA is responsible for admissions, but must consult the governing body. The LEA has a role in the coordination of admissions procedures.	Governors determine the policy after consultation with the LEA and other admission authorities. They make the decision on which pupils to admit. The LEA has a role in the coordination of admissions procedures.
Advice	LEA chief education officer has certain rights to attend governing body meetings to give advice. diocesan director of education has parallel rights.	LEA chief education officer has certain rights to attend governing body meetings to give advice. Governors may give similar rights to the diocesan director of education.	LEA chief education officer has certain rights to attend governing body meetings to give advice. Governors may give similar rights to the diocesan director of education.

Inspection	OFSTED inspectors look at most issues. Section 23 inspectors inspect RE, worship and school ethos (SMSC).	OFSTED inspectors look at general issues and RE. Section 23 inspectors inspect worship and reserved RE teaching if it is provided and may report on school ethos (SMSC).	OFSTED inspectors look at general issues and RE. Section 23 inspectors inspect worship and reserved RE teaching if it is provided and may report on school ethos (SMSC).

Notes on the tables

Voluntary aided schools

In these schools the Church has a majority of the governors. This should make it possible for there to be clear Christian leadership in all areas of the conduct of the school. This will depend, however, on the extent to which the governors are able to establish and maintain a policy for the appointment of teachers that ensures sufficient teachers with a clear Christian commitment.

Voluntary controlled and foundation schools

The balance on the governing body between the various groups who nominate governors mirrors the partnerships that should exist within a Church school. The fact that there is no group with a majority on the governing body can be an incentive to ensure that the school moves forward through consensus.

Buildings

While trustees own the buildings, it is for the governing body to ensure that they are well maintained and improved, where and when necessary. How this work is funded depends on the category of the school (see preceding sections). The principles, however, are the same for all schools.

- Schools must be safe places for staff and pupils to work in and for parents and others to visit.

- Maintenance delayed creates larger bills later.

- All work should be undertaken within the framework created by the asset management plan (AMP) for the school.

- A qualified architect or surveyor should supervise major repair work and all improvements; usually this person or organization will develop a long-term working relationship with the governing body.

- If volunteers are used to carry out some of the tasks, their work should be supervised by someone who is professionally competent and care should be taken to ensure that the work is completed to the highest possible standard.

- When an outside contractor is employed to undertake work on a school building, the firm should be competent to do the work and carry appropriate insurance.

In one of the points above reference was made to the asset management plan. The LEA will have produced an asset management plan for all the school buildings in its area. The governors of each school need to use this basic information to produce their own building development plan for their school. This plan will identify a schedule for recurring maintenance, such as external redecoration, and an outline of how the school buildings might be developed to ensure that they provide the best possible environment in which to educate the pupils and in which staff can work. The LEA building development plan covers issues of the building's state of repair, its ability to accommodate the number of pupils now on roll or expected in the future and the suitability of the teaching and other facilities for their task. The asset management plan for the school should reflect the same priorities.

The existence of an LEA asset management plan is designed to ensure that Government grants are targeted to those schools in greatest need.

Insurance

All schools need to carry a range of insurance cover. Most of this is provided or arranged through Local Education Authorities. Schools need to be satisfied that they have a clear understanding of what insurance the LEA provides.

Governors of voluntary aided schools are advised to have their own insurance for the buildings for which they have responsibility. This is usually arranged through the diocese as a block policy. One or two LEAs arrange this cover for their schools. During periods when major building work is being undertaken in the school, additional cover will be necessary.

Governors of all Church schools must ensure that they have, or know that the LEA or DBE has on their behalf, a public liability policy related essentially to access the public may have, whether authorized, unofficial, casual or even unlawful, to the school premises. Governors of voluntary aided and foundation schools have additional responsibilities as employers of staff. They must have, or know that the LEA or DBE has on their behalf, employers' liability insurance. They are also advised to have, or know that the LEA or DBE has on their behalf, legal expenses insurance so that they can be properly supported in law over anything that might arise. Most dioceses have made appropriate arrangements for their schools in this area. Insurance for schools is an area of rapid change and development. Before making any changes to their policies, governors or the head should discuss the issues with their diocese and LEA. At the time of writing the DfES is preparing detailed guidance to provide clarity and consistency of practice across the country.

Change of category

From time to time it would be appropriate for schools to consider whether they are in the most appropriate category for their circumstances. Schools should not change category too often but should identify that category which is most appropriate in order to ensure that they can operate effectively as a Church school. Any school considering a change of category should consult its diocesan director of education at an early stage.

Some of the possible changes are:

Voluntary controlled to voluntary aided

There are a number of schools who have completed this change since the passage of the School Standards and Framework Act 1998. Before this Act this change was only possible in very limited circumstances. Since 1986 the change from controlled to aided was only possible if the governors compensated the LEA for the full amount which they had spent on improving, remodelling or replacing the building. No grant was available from the Department for this purpose. The change is now a much easier proposition. Any compensation due, and compensation can only arise in limited circumstances, is only payable out of the proceeds of sale of the school building after the school has closed.

The procedure for change of category involves local consultation, the publication of public notices and approval by the School Organization Committee/National Assembly for Wales. This Committee will require evidence that the governing body, with appropriate support, can meet the financial obligations for a voluntary aided school. It will be clear that this change is unlikely to be effected without the active support and involvement of the diocese.

Voluntary aided to voluntary controlled

The arrangements for this move were changed by the 1998 Act. Previously the governing body could simply resolve to seek approval from the Secretary of State. Some governing bodies did so when faced with a significant bill for repairs or improvements, apparently unaware of the help that was available to them from their diocese. Since 1998 the governing body must publish formal proposals to change its category, in the same way that any other change would have to be conducted.

Voluntary controlled or voluntary aided to foundation

This might seem to be an attractive move for some schools in view of the 100 per cent funding from the LEA for capital projects and the greater apparent freedom over some issues, but it is clear from elsewhere in this book that foundation schools do not have the same religious freedoms as voluntary aided schools.

Other moves

Now that foundation schools have had a few years to explore how they fit into the local education system it may be that a number of foundation schools will want to consider whether a change of category to voluntary aided would be in the best interests of the school. Governors considering such a move should explore the advantages and disadvantages in consultation with their diocese.

No Church school can become a community school without a total closure of the school. The LEA would have to acquire the building and open a new school on the premises. The same is true for travel in the opposite direction from community school to Church school, a journey, however, being considered and taken by a number of schools.

Finance

The earlier chapter on governors provided an introduction to some of the financial issues that concern governors and school leaders. In this section the focus is on the financial implications of the school buildings. In voluntary aided schools the governing body must be prepared to find at least 10 per cent of the cost of capital work on the buildings that are its responsibility. It is supported in this by the Diocesan Board of Education and may sometimes be able to draw upon trust funds held for the purpose of supporting voluntary aided schools. The governing body must also insure their building and users of the building on those occasions when they give permission for it to be used for purposes other than the provision of education within the orbit of the Local Education Authority. Any income gained from these lettings, after payment into the school's funds of any costs incurred against that budget, is available to the governing body to use to support its work and responsibilities.

This chapter has focused on issues that can seem remote from the education of children. Governors and headteachers need to ensure that they have addressed the issues properly so that they have appropriate solutions for their school. If the category and buildings are right, all the energy can be focused on the quality of education. Where they are wrong they raise issues that dominate people's agenda and distract from concern for the needs of the pupils.

115

Specific guidance on the change from voluntary controlled to voluntary aided and other issues raised in this chapter can be found on www.churchschools.co.uk.

The civil framework for Church schools: national and local government

> A strong and developing partnership between the Church and LEAs is at the heart of our proposals for an increase in the provision of Church schools. The Church and the LEAs have had a long and productive relationship characterized by a spirit of cooperation and genuine debate on the nature and purpose of denominational provision.
>
> *The Way Ahead*, paragraph 4.22

The context within which Church schools operate is created by a partnership between local and central government and the Churches at local and national level. This chapter will explore the governmental aspects of that partnership and the following chapter will deal with the Church dimension. Those involved in leading Church schools need to be aware of the ways in which the various agencies locally and nationally work together and share responsibilities. This is important in order to understand how the work of their individual school relates to these partnerships and where they can best turn for help and support in particular circumstances.

Central government

The role of central government and its agencies is to create the overall framework for schools, set standards, provide effective support and monitoring and ensure that there is a high-quality flow of recruits into the teaching profession. In recent years it has also taken responsibility for setting standards for professional development for teachers. It achieves these tasks through legislation and the work of government departments and agencies.

The framework

The major legislation that affects schools is contained in the two Acts of 1996, the School Standards and Framework Act 1998, the Learning and Skills Act 2000 and the Education Act 2002. The 1996 Acts consolidated education law passed between 1944 and 1995; thus, although there have been many changes, much of the education system that we have inherited owes its origins to an Education Act passed in wartime. It is remarkable that, despite the pressures of wartime, the 1944 Act was passed only after a considerable period of consultation and following considerable negotiations between Government and the Churches. The principles established in 1944 have continued to inform the way in which education in this country has developed ever since. Education law requires that all children should receive a period of formal education between the ages of 5 and 16. Increasingly, provision is made for younger children to receive some education appropriate to their age if their parents wish them to participate. Similarly, many young people choose to stay on at school or in further education beyond the statutory school age of 16. The law does not require schools to serve defined age groups and, since 1944, a mixed pattern of provision has grown up in different parts of the country, reflecting the decisions taken within particular Local Education Authorities. Broadly speaking, however, there are three bands into which the statutory provision of education is divided:

- primary, which is understood to encompass all education up to the end of the academic year in which the child reaches the age of 11 (Year 6);

- secondary, which encompasses the rest of a young person's schooling, whether this ends at 16 (Year 11) or 18;

- tertiary, which covers education offered in tertiary or further education colleges (higher education in colleges or universities falls outside the scope of this book).

Primary and secondary education are the responsibility of Local Education Authorities; tertiary education is funded through local Learning and Skills Councils. In some parts of the country, schools are not separated into distinctively primary and secondary but include an intermediate or middle school stage. The advent of the national curriculum, introduced after the Education Reform Act of 1988, which provided a curriculum structure of key stages, two corresponding to the primary phase and two to the secondary (to age 16), has created a new pressure, which is leading some authorities to review the future of middle schools. Broadly speaking, the division into primary, secondary and tertiary has existed since 1944. The School Standards and Framework Act 1998, while not changing these broad bands, did provide for changes in the categories of schools, which affect the way in which they are governed and the responsibilities of individual governing bodies. There are three broad categories for schools, regardless of whether they are primary schools, secondary schools or serving an age group within or across these two broad bands. The categories are community school, foundation school and voluntary school. Within the voluntary category there are subdivisions into voluntary aided and voluntary controlled. Details of the major differences between these types of school were given in the previous chapter.

The government agencies

At present the Government has two main agencies that have an impact on what is taught in schools. As its name implies, the Qualifications and Curriculum Authority has a responsibility for the public examinations taken by pupils in schools as a measure of their progress at the ages of 7, 11 and 14 and to gain formal qualifications either at GCSE or A/S and A2 level at 16, 17 and 18. It is also responsible for advising Government on the content of the national curriculum subjects and for providing support materials that show how the non-statutory subjects can interrelate with content that is required by law. The only exception to this framework is religious education which, because it has been a statutory requirement for far longer than the national curriculum subjects, has the content of the curriculum determined locally rather than nationally. The Qualifications and Curriculum Authority has provided materials for religious education that are intended to be a resource for the local authority conferences that have responsibility for the subject. If a national framework for religious education is developed this will be done under the auspices of the Qualifications and Curriculum Authority. These functions are carried out in Wales by Awdurdod Cymysterau, Cwricwlwm Acasesu Cymru, Qualifications, Curriculum and Assessment Authority for Wales (ACCAC).

The other agency involved in curriculum issues is the Office for Standards in Education (OFSTED), which is responsible for the inspection of all schools in England and for providing advice to Government on the development of education, based on its inspection evidence. In Wales these duties are carried out by ESTYN, formerly known as the Office of Her Majesty's Chief Inspector (OHMCI). In Church schools OFSTED/ESTYN does not have complete responsibility. Those aspects of education that are determined by the school's trust deed are not inspected by an OFSTED/ESTYN appointed inspector but by one appointed by the governors as a fit person to inspect the denominational aspects of the school. The National Society has provided a national training scheme and framework for the inspection of Anglican schools (see next chapter for details).

There are three major agencies intimately involved with teaching, teacher education and professional development. The oldest of these is the Teacher Training Agency. The task of this agency is to ensure that there is a steady supply of high-quality, well-trained entrants into the teaching profession. In order to achieve this, it takes initiatives designed to encourage recruitment to the profession, sets standards for the training of new entrants and promotes a variety of routes into the profession and ways in which this training can be delivered.

The responsibility for setting standards for the further professional development of teachers after qualification lies with the National College for School Leadership. The major programmes of the college are training for subject leaders, a National Professional Qualification for Headteachers (NPQH), an induction programme for newly appointed headteachers, currently called 'Headlamp', and a Leadership Programme for Serving Headteachers (LPSH). Details of how these programmes are developing and how they can meet the needs of those exercising these different levels of responsibility within Church schools can be found on the National Society's web site.

The third body is the General Teaching Council for England (there is a separate GTC for Wales). These bodies are responsible for issues associated with the registration of teachers as members of the profession and the professional standards that teachers are expected to demonstrate in their work. All teachers working in maintained schools must be registered with the appropriate General Teaching Council. These councils also promote professional development for teachers by offering bursaries.

The Department for Education and Skills/National Assembly for Wales not only set standards for schools through the work of their agencies; they also set standards for Local Education Authorities and, working with their agencies, undertake monitoring and inspection of the work of LEAs and scrutiny of some of their major schemes and policies.

Local Education Authorities

The Local Education Authority is responsible for providing the funding for schools in their area from council tax and from the money allocated to them from central government. While the authority may retain some funds for work designed to administer the system and support the development of high-quality education within their schools, the majority of the funding is delegated directly to the governing body of each school. This enables schools to make budget decisions in ways that most directly benefit the education of the pupils in their school. The Local Education Authorities' responsibilities are not limited to financial affairs. They have to provide a number of services designed to meet the needs of individual pupils and a range of policy documents intended to set appropriate local standards and ensure that these are delivered. In their relationships with schools LEAs must operate within a centrally developed code of practice. In order to work with their schools and others concerned with education, the Local Education Authority will create a number of forums, committee and other meetings. Among the most important, in terms of their impact on Church schools, are the following.

The Education Overview and Scrutiny Committee

This title should be taken to indicate a description of the work of the committee or committees within the structure of local government adopted by the local authority. The actual committee(s) covering this work may be titled differently. The majority of members will be elected councillors but there will be members with full voting rights from the Churches and the parent body. Teachers may also have representation on the committee but without the right to vote.

School Organization Committee (SOC)

This committee exercises powers formerly belonging to the Secretary of State by bringing together the various groups interested in school organization at local level: the LEA, schools, the Anglican and the Roman Catholic dioceses and, where there are post-16 implications, the local Learning and Skills Council. It provides a forum in which the Local Education Authority's plans for the development of schools in its area can be discussed and, if the committee is so minded, approved. The main issues that will come to a School Organization Committee are authority plans for the reorganization of schools, school closures or the creation of new schools to meet the demand for more places. There are no School Organization Committees in Wales; the Local Education Authorities undertake their duties.

Standing Advisory Council for Religious Education (SACRE)

This council brings together those bodies in the authority with a particular interest in religious education and school worship. It has the responsibility for advising the local authority on these issues and taking initiatives to promote religious education and school worship in the area. It has a particular interest in the use of the Local Authority's agreed syllabus for religious education and a duty to inform the local authority if the syllabus needs revision. It does not have responsibility for school worship in Church schools or religious education undertaken in Church schools in accordance with the school's trust deed.

Agreed syllabus conference

If the local authority decides that its agreed syllabus for religious education needs revision, it must convene a conference for this purpose. The constitution of this agreed syllabus conference is

123

different from that of a Standing Advisory Council for religious education because there can be no co-opted members. Despite this difference, in many authorities the membership of the two bodies is almost identical. The conference only exists for the period of time that it takes to generate a new religious education syllabus for the authority and for this to receive approval by the local authority.

Early Years Development and Childcare Partnerships

These bring together all the parties concerned or involved with the provision of education for children up to the age of 14. They are charged with the responsibility of advising the authority on the best strategies to ensure that there are an adequate number of places for children whose parents wish them to have education before they reach statutory school age.

Admissions Forum

The Local Education Authority must bring together representatives of all admissions authorities in order to discuss the coordination and administration of school admission and transfer between schools at whatever age this takes place. As well as the local authorities and the churches, there will be representatives of voluntary aided and foundation schools on the Admissions Forum because the governing bodies in these schools are the admission authority for the school. In some areas, neighbouring Local Education Authorities may also be represented on the Admissions Forum where there are a significant number of cross-border admissions.

Schools Forum

These forums will consist mainly of elected representatives of the schools in an LEA and will provide a means whereby the LEA's arrangements for financial delegation and other related matters can be discussed. At the time of writing there is no formal experience of these forums as they are a creation of the Education Act 2002. It will be important that, in authorities where there are voluntary or foundation schools, their voice is heard on these forums so that, within an overall policy that establishes and maintains fairness between different schools, the needs of all schools, with their different legal responsibilities, are properly taken into account.

A prime duty of the Local Education Authority is to act for school improvement and therefore much of the work that they do with schools and the services that they provide has this objective in mind.

European institutions

The European Union and the Council of Europe both have interests in education throughout the areas that they cover. The latter has a particular interest in maintaining a Europe-wide standard on human rights. They promote European under-standing, programmes of learning and visits. Many Church schools, both at primary and secondary level, are becoming involved in such programmes.

Organizations and associations of teachers

These fall into two distinct categories. The first category is pro-fessional associations concerned with issues related to employ-ment and professional responsibilities and duties. Most teachers belong to one of these professional associations and teachers can consult local and regional representatives over issues of concern. At the school level, representatives of these associations should be facilitated in carrying out their tasks on behalf of their members.

The other form of professional association of teachers is one that brings together teachers with a particular subject or phase interest. Some of these associations have a national structure and standing and make a major contribution to the continuing development of their subject or phase. Other groupings have a more local nature and serve as a forum for local professional development and curriculum action. This may be as simple as coordinating school sports fixtures and facilitating teams to represent the schools at LEA or regional level, or include such complex tasks as organizing national or international conferences for teachers with a particular interest and commitment to a single subject area. Many of these subject associations have come together at national level to create the College of Teachers, which exists to promote high standards of education and professional development amongst all members of the profession. Many Church schools benefit significantly from the participation of their teachers in such local or national associations.

More details of all the issues raised in this chapter can be found on www.churchschools.co.uk.

The ecclesiastical framework for Church schools: the local and national Church

> The General Synod and the Archbishops' Council have identified Church schools as standing at the centre of the Church's mission to the nation. Our work over the last eighteen months has confirmed the crucial importance of Church schools to the whole mission of the Church to children and young people, and indeed to the long-term well-being of the Church of England.
>
> *The Way Ahead*, Executive Summary, paragraph 1

In the previous chapter some of the framework of central and local government was outlined insofar as it affects the work of Church schools. Church schools not only relate to central and local government, they also have an important relationship with the Church by which they were established and whose practice and traditions of education they have a duty to reflect.

The Church locally

The support for education in the Church of England and the Church in Wales is organized locally at three distinct but complementary levels.

The local parish

The Anglican Church is based on a parochial system that covers the entire country. Each parish has a distinctive geographical boundary and the parish priest is given responsibility by the bishop for the population within that boundary. The parish priest also has a number of responsibilities with regard to arrangements for Anglican worship and the supervision of the use of Anglican buildings within the parish. These responsibilities include a responsibility for the collective worship in a Church school, as this will reflect the Anglican tradition. This is normally exercised through the priest's membership of the governing body, where policy on school worship will be discussed. It is particularly important in those schools that celebrate the Eucharist as part of their pattern of worship, that the policy of the school makes it clear what restrictions, if any, are required on who may be invited to be the celebrant at the Eucharist. The only exceptions to this general oversight exercised by the parish priest are where the school has been specifically licensed by the bishop. In every parish there are a Parochial Church Council and a number of church-wardens. Should there be a vacancy for an incumbent (inter-regnum), the churchwardens automatically take over a number of the parish priest's responsibilities but not those related to the Church school. Historically, when Anglican schools were founded, the trustees of the building were often the vicar and churchwardens of the parish in which the school was situated. Many of the more modern schools now have trust deeds in which the diocese is the trustee of the school, but where the school was founded in the nineteenth century the trustees were either named individuals, in which case the trust deed may need re-establishing, or, more usually, the holders of the major parochial offices.

Where there is a Church school in the parish, the Parochial Church Council may have been given responsibility for nominat-ing a proportion of the foundation governors on the governing body by the Instrument of Government. The PCC may decide to include the headteacher of the school in its own membership. This can only be achieved by co-option and such a co-option would depend on the headteacher's being an actual communicant of the Anglican Church. Where such arrangements have been established, it can be a sign of good mutual collaboration and confidence between the school and the parish in which it is set. Sometimes, as a result of historic agreements possibly deriving from school reorganization or the closure of neighbouring schools, other local Parochial Church Councils may also be given the responsibility of nominating governors on to the governing body of a Church school.

The deanery

The next level of organization beyond the parish is the deanery. The deanery is led by a rural or area dean, who is one of the senior parochial clergy in the area, chosen by the bishop after consultation with the other clergy of the area. The deanery also brings together elected members representing each of the Anglican churches in the deanery to a meeting known as a deanery synod in England and a deanery conference in Wales. Because of the wide area that they serve, a few Anglican secondary schools in England are closely related to the deanery and the deanery synod for the area. In such cases the deanery synod is likely to have the responsibility for nominating some of the foundation governors.

The diocese in England

Beyond the deanery is the diocese, which is led by the diocesan bishop. There is also a body of elected representatives of the Church called the diocesan synod, which exists to consider matters concerning the Church of England and to make provision for such matters in relation to their diocese, and to consider and express their opinion on any other matter of religious or public interest; to advise the bishop of any matters upon which he may consult the synod; and to consider and express their opinion on any matter referred to them by the General Synod. Responsibility for diocesan finances is held by the Diocesan Board of Finance. Under the Diocesan Boards of Education Measure 1991, every diocese in

129

England is required to have a Diocesan Board of Education with a diocesan director of education as its principal officer. This committee has a number of responsibilities in respect of the Church's involvement in statutory education and in particular its support for Anglican schools and for religious education and school worship in all schools. The Diocesan Board of Education may well employ specialist staff, as well as the diocesan director of education, to support and help Church schools in matters of building, curriculum and school management. This team of people provides a very important source of support for Church schools in addition to that available from the Local Education Authority. Normally, very close working relationships exist between the Local Education Authority and the Diocesan Board of Education. The diocesan director of education and other members of the diocesan education team are responsible to the Diocesan Board of Education for the work that they do on its behalf. The Diocesan Board of Education must make a report to the diocesan synod of the work it has undertaken on behalf of the diocese. For the most part the relationship between the diocesan director of education, the Diocesan Board of Education and individual Church schools is a matter of advice and cooperation. Under certain limited circumstances the Diocesan Board of Education can give direction to a particular governing body if it believes the governing body is acting against the interests of its own Church school or all Church schools in general. There are clearly defined circumstances in which this power can be used and if the Diocesan Board of Education decides to use it, it must report what it has done to the diocesan synod. In other cases, before making a final decision, the governing body may have to seek the advice of the Diocesan Board of Education, and have regard to that advice when making its decisions. The Education Act 2002 extends this duty for a voluntary aided school to the consideration of its admissions policy.

Every Diocesan Board of Education sets its own priorities and responds to the needs of the schools in its area in ways that most closely reflect their needs and the limits of the resources that are available. Many Diocesan Boards of Education provide training for governors and senior staff of Church schools and for RE and worship coordinators in all schools. Some Diocesan Boards of Education provide religious education centres open to all interested teachers. The responsibilities of Diocesan Boards of Education are usually not limited to schools; they often include the Church's work in further and higher education and may extend to the Church's educational work in the parishes. This last area of work may fall under one of the other boards, councils or committees of the diocesan synod, if it has not been felt appropriate to include it within the brief of the Diocesan Board of Education.

The diocese in Wales

In Wales, the Diocesan Boards of Education Measure 1991 does not apply. Nevertheless, each diocese has a diocesan director of education who reports to the diocesan bishop through a board or similar body. Their teams offer support to schools in much the same way as their counterparts in England.

The diocesan bishop is responsible for Church schools in the diocese and he delegates the discharge of that responsibility to the diocesan director of education.

General

It is important for all Church schools to seek to maintain good relationships with the diocesan director of education and the diocesan education team and it would be very surprising if there were an Anglican school that did not have a well-established pattern of contact with its local diocese. If issues about the nature of worship in Anglican schools or of religious education in Anglican voluntary aided schools arise within the school's staff, governing body or parents, the source of advice and guidance and the person to whom appeals can be made and who can decide on complaints related to these issues is the diocesan bishop. In most dioceses, however, the bishop would expect the issues to be referred to the diocesan director of education in the first instance. The diocesan director will ensure that there is a sufficient level of support material in these particular areas of Anglican school work to provide a clear basis for guidance to schools. The endorsement of this guidance by the diocesan bishop is a strong indication of the view that he is likely to take, if appealed to for a decision on any issue in the above areas.

The Church nationally

Beyond the diocese the Church is organized in provinces, which are groups of dioceses under the leadership of an archbishop. There is, therefore, a province of Wales and, in England, provinces of York and Canterbury. In England much of the national work is carried out by the General Synod, which brings together representatives of both English provinces, and by the Archbishops' Council, which has responsibility for the direction of the Church's national work. Reporting to the Archbishops' Council is the Church of England Board of Education, which has the responsibility for representing the Church at national level in matters of education. One of its principal tasks on behalf of Church schools is to represent their interests nationally, particularly with the Department for Education and Skills at times of education legislation. The Church of England Board of Education is responsible for developing policy that has been approved by the Archbishops' Council and the General Synod. The education policy of the Church in Wales is developed in consultation between the diocesan directors of education and the bench of bishops.

The National Society

The educational work of the Anglican Church in the provinces of England and Wales benefits from the support of the National Society. This Anglican charity was founded in 1811 for the purpose of promoting Church schools. Its full name, according to the most recent of its royal charters, is the National Society (Church of England) for Promoting Religious Education. As it was the first national society for any purpose to be granted a royal charter, it has the privilege of being able to be known simply as The National Society. The Society works very closely with the Church of England Board of Education and the Church in Wales to support the work of Church schools and religious education, school worship and spiritual, moral, social and cultural development in all schools. It does this through courses offered in collaboration with the Church Colleges of Higher Education, through managing the section 23 inspection process in Anglican schools and through providing a religious education centre of national standing in London. Many of the senior officers of the National Society are joint appointments with the Church of England Board of Education. The National Society in support of Church schools maintains a specialist web site for Church school governance and management to which this book is an introduction.

More details of all the issues raised in this chapter can be found on www.churchschools.co.uk.

Index

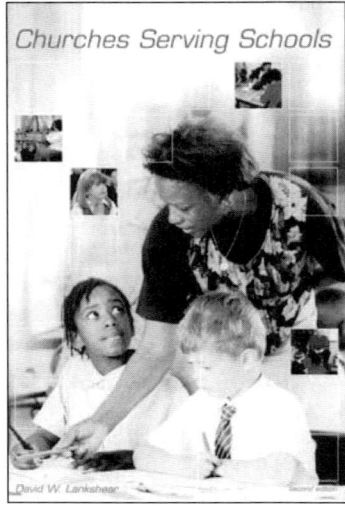

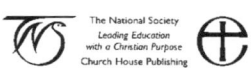

FREE WEB SITE FOR SCHOOLS!

www.natsoc.org.uk provides a range of resources and guidance for all who are involved in education. The web site now includes the material from www.churchschools.co.uk, previously a subscription-only site.

Whether you are a headteacher, teacher, governor, parent or just interesed in education, you will find the site to be an invaluable resource.

What will be on the web site?

The web site at www.natsoc.org.uk will provide:

- Hundreds of pages of management guidance and legal advice on areas ranging from governing Church schools to staffing procedures and the curriculum;

- Material on collective worship and RE;

- Pro forma contracts and application forms;

- Regular updates on how the Church is supporting Church schools by implementing the recommendations of *The Way ahead*;

- General advice for parents (including information on admissions and the distinctiveness of Church schools);

- Resources supporting the vocation to teach;

- Ideas to help churches to support their local schools:

- Material supporting the Church Colleges Certificate in Church School Studies;

- Information on the work of The National Society.

www.natsoc.org.uk